YOUNG GUNS

OBSESSION, OVERWATCH, AND THE FUTURE OF GAMING

AUSTIN MOORHEAD

hachette
BOOKS

NEW YORK

To Mom and Dad

Hachette Books
Hachette Book Group
1290 Avenue of the Americas
New York, NY 10104
hachettebookgroup.com
twitter.com/hachettebooks
instagram.com/hachettebooks

First Edition: March 2020

Hachette Books is a division of Hachette Book Group, Inc.

The Hachette Books name and logo are trademarks of Hachette Book Group, Inc.

The publisher is not responsible for websites (or their content) that are not owned by the publisher.

The Hachette Speakers Bureau provides a wide range of authors for speaking events. To find out more, go to www.hachettespeakersbureau.com or call (866) 376-6591.

Print book interior design by Six Red Marbles, Inc.

Library of Congress Control Number: 2020931304

ISBNs: 978-0-316-42138-6 (trade paperback), 978-0-316-42139-3 (ebook)

Printed in the United States of America

LSC-C

10 9 8 7 6 5 4 3 2 1

CONTENTS

CHAPTER 1

THE PITCH

Bobby Kotick, CEO of Activision-Blizzard, a $7 billion revenue video-game company known for titles such as *World of Warcraft, Starcraft, Diablo,* and *Call of Duty,* invited four men to join him at his enormous birch conference table. He moved around the room with ease, smiling as he circled the table to shake hands. That Bobby was comfortable here in the boardroom was no accident—it was the same room where he'd updated Activision-Blizzard's directors on the state of the business for the past twenty-six years; over that span, out of more than a hundred quarterly earnings releases, he'd had to deliver bad news—missed quarterly earnings estimates—only six times.

"Gentlemen, welcome." Bobby spoke just loud enough

to be heard, causing his guests to lean forward slightly as they listened. "If you could each please have a seat where those two pieces of paper are laid out..." In front of four of the seats on one side of the conference table, two pieces of paper lay side by side, facedown. "Don't turn them over just yet."

There was some shuffling as the men arranged themselves. Bobby raised a hand in what was almost a wave, almost a pointing motion. "I see you've brought Brett along with you, which I'm very happy to see. Brett's great. He really gets it. We've heard such wonderful things about Brett."

The Brett in question, Brett Lautenbach, was twenty-eight years old. Though he was the youngest man in the room by twenty years, he was familiar with the rule of black sheep. Raised in what he described as "an idyllic town in the Midwest," Naperville, a western suburb of Chicago, Brett was born into an IBM family and became the first man in his family's memory to opt *not* to work for the company. His father had worked there for his entire career, as had four of Brett's uncles, one of whom was once part of the four-person management committee that ran IBM and a rumored candidate to become CEO. Bill Gates once accused another of the Lautenbach brothers of conducting a smear campaign against Windows 95. Despite descending from IBM royalty, Brett developed a different passion very early in life: film. When he followed that passion to New York University's film school, he discovered he had a knack for corralling creative types: helping them schedule, budget, connect with the right people, and run a tight ship. In another time line, Brett would probably be an associate film producer, but in this time line he found himself in the Activision-Blizzard boardroom for the most important meeting of his young life.

Brett was there in the capacity of president of NRG Esports, and he was the principal reason that the company's three owners were currently sitting to his left at Bobby's table. Brett's ass was on the line in this meeting, and his anxieties were building. During his interviews for the NRG job, he'd pitched buying a team in the new esports league that Blizzard was basing on their new hit game, *Overwatch*, as the central building block of NRG's future. NRG had just suffered an ignominious dethronement as the reigning king of esports leagues, the League of Legends Championship Series (LCS), and an Overwatch League (OWL) team could be the new crown jewel of the NRG portfolio. After little more than dipping a toe in the esports business, Blizzard was putting unprecedented effort and money into developing the Overwatch League, with a vision of one day rivaling traditional sports leagues in size and profitability. Upon release, *Overwatch* had immediately become a sensationally popular first-person-shooter (FPS) video game.

The game was novel in that it combined the best aspects of games like *League of Legends*—unique heroes with distinct abilities working on a six-person team—with the excellent gameplay, well-developed story, and rich artistic design that were hallmarks of Blizzard games.

Brett had hounded the league's commissioner to help land this meeting, finally tracking him down at a whiskey bar in Shanghai. He took it as a good sign that Bobby, the CEO of *Overwatch*'s parent company himself, was running it. Yet, however close he thought he was to landing a deal that'd give NRG a team in OWL, Brett needed the men he'd brought with him to see the light. And as a few bullet points from their resumes illustrated, they were not easy to impress. Andy Miller, one of the three NRG cofounders at the meeting with Brett, had learned to set high standards from one of the most famously demanding CEOs in history. Andy had cofounded an ad network company called Quattro Wireless in 2006, which he sold to Apple three years later for $275 million. Andy then worked directly for Steve Jobs for two years. After leaving Apple and running another tech company for a few years, he had an opportunity to acquire a partial stake in the NBA's Sacramento Kings and would serve on the league's internal digital committee. Shortly after, in 2015, he cofounded NRG. Mark Mastrov, another of the NRG cofounders, started 24 Hour Fitness in 1983 and sold it in 2005 for $1.6 billion. He'd joined the

Sacramento Kings and NRG ownership groups in partnership with Andy. Jeff Glass, the final NRG cofounder, had sold his own mobile ad company for $250 million. As Brett said, "These guys are geniuses."

Why were these tech zillionaires meeting to discuss buying esports teams when they could have been doing anything with their fortunes? Though their answers varied, their passion for competition and games emerged frequently. "I just love sports," Andy explained to me. "I'm a kid from Boston who was obsessed with sports my whole life. I played it, I watched it, I wanted to own the Red Sox, still do. When I graduated, by some miracle, near the top of my law school class, I had my pick of law firms, so I went to the firm that represented the Red Sox. When I got lucky and sold a couple companies and moved out here with some money, I bought into the Rockies' minor league baseball team, the Single A team in Modesto: the Nuts. And I loved it. Then I met up with Mark Mastrov and got involved with the group that was going to buy the Kings. And I wanted to run everything. Then I saw this opportunity with esports."

For someone like Andy who seemed able to achieve anything in his unlikely career—from start-ups to the Kings and now perhaps esports—it was important to always work with the best people. In that respect, he'd been anxious about Brett the first time they met. They'd planned to rendezvous in the Theme Building in LAX, but because it was closed off they went to a basement employee cafeteria. Andy decided the relocation would be a good test to see how chill Brett was about chaos and change, long-time hallmarks, it seemed, of the esports world. They were somehow swiped through the cafeteria's security, assumed to be custodians, and enjoyed their grilled cheeses in what Andy described as a "semi-abandoned" setting.

How did Brett dress for this big meeting with Andy? In what Andy described as a "little hipster outfit" that he would be, as NRG's resident hipster, lovingly mocked for frequently wearing. Beyond the dark sunglasses, it consisted of a button-down shirt with at least one button undone and a camel-hair blazer. Andy would come to consider that this was his "go-to blazer."

A passion for the games he's helped build was also the reason Brett was meeting with Activision-Blizzard and not toiling away at IBM's headquarters. He combined that love for actual gameplay with a love for business. In his role as president of NRG Esports, Brett had to be able to impress the CMO of a Fortune 100 company and also shoot the shit with a teenage pro gaming prospect. In one sense, the bank account sense, Brett did not belong in Activision-Blizzard's boardroom. But in another sense, he did. To hear Andy tell it, "Brett's the most hard-working guy I've ever met."

Hard work, however, didn't necessarily translate to schmoozing the most powerful man in video games, and with Bobby indicating that he would invite other Blizzard employees into the room to present the league, those skills seemed to be what was needed to get a conversation started. Brett knew that other esports organizations had already sat at this table to hear this exact pitch and that NRG were both newer to esports and had a scarlet letter around their neck: their League of Legends team had been demoted from the LCS.

Andy rose to the call. "I think we have something in common," he said to Bobby. "I remember reading somewhere that you were sort of an apprentice under Steve Jobs. Is that right? I worked for Steve for a couple of years."

"When I was in my twenties, Steve Jobs convinced me to quit college," Bobby said. "I left college to make software for Apple."

Brett felt the conversation flickering, so he chimed in, "What is it like?"

"It's terrifying," Andy said. "Amazing, terrifying."

"When you knew it was him on the phone," Bobby said, "it was like 'oh gosh here we go.'"

"Yeah," Andy said. "Every time you talked to him. There was no winging anything. You had to be incredibly well thought out and incredibly concise. You had to have a 360 understanding of the world that your conversation or decision touched. Otherwise, he didn't have time for quote-unquote bozos."

"Oh yes, the bozos," said Bobby. It was famously one of Jobs's favorite terms.

"I remember," Andy said. "He would say to me that he didn't hire me, he bought me, so I have to become an Apple person."

Bobby nodded, and he and Andy fell silent for a moment.

The important negotiation points between NRG and the Overwatch League had yet to come up, but Brett felt that the meeting was off to a good start. Strong business relationships begin with strong personal relationships, and the connection of shared experience could only help legitimize NRG as a potential team owner. If Bobby thought NRG was legit, then Brett knew the meeting would succeed: Bobby was eager to make a deal. Activision-Blizzard had announced the Overwatch League at 2016's BlizzCon, the 30,000-person annual event that lets fans hear the biggest announcements for Blizzard games live, play Blizzard games on the thousands of PCs set up there, listen to the people who make the games talk about how they made them (and, in 2016 anyway, watch "Weird Al" Yankovic perform). Tickets cost $200 and BlizzCon sold out every year. *Overwatch* had been released six months earlier, in May 2016, on PC, PlayStation, and Xbox, and sold more than 20 million copies before the year was out, making it the best-selling new game of 2016. The second-best-selling new game of 2016 was Activision's *Call of Duty: Infinite Warfare.* Now it was March 2017, and with no announcements about team owners or the inaugural season's start date, the rumor was that Blizzard was behind on their goal to launch that fall. Which was a little odd, given the people with whom Bobby had been talking.

At the 2016 BlizzCon, Bobby had given an initial pitch of the Overwatch League to a group of potential owners behind the scenes. Those in attendance included titans of the NFL, NBA, and Silicon Valley. Among them: Robert Kraft, owner of the New England Patriots; Stan Kroenke, owner of the Los Angeles Rams and Arsenal FC; Joe Lacob and Peter Guber, owners of the Golden State Warriors; Wesley Edens, owner of the Milwaukee Bucks; Elon Musk, CEO of SpaceX and Tesla; and Jack Etienne, owner of Cloud9, who would eventually buy the London Overwatch League franchise. The only person in the room with esports experience was Jack Etienne, who described the meeting as defined by the nervousness he felt talking with "all these billionaire dudes" because, in his words, "these guys are badasses." When I asked Jack whether they told him why they invited him, he said that it was because they "recognized the mark we'd made in esports and thought it'd be good for the league for teams that have been a part of esports for a long time, and done really well, to be a part of it." Having Cloud9's owner involved would indeed prove validating for the league. Putting his nervousness talking with the likes of Stan Kroenke and Elon Musk aside, Jack was sold on the concept. He remembered that, as he left BlizzCon 2016, he thought, "I'm gonna do this," and the only question he had remaining was how much it would cost and how he would come up with the money.

As it turned out, NRG was not invited—by Bobby or anyone else—to BlizzCon 2016. Though already sporting celebrity investors such as Shaquille O'Neal, Michael Strahan, Alex Rodriguez, and Jennifer Lopez, NRG was less than a year old, and in that short time, they'd already suffered the single greatest disaster that can befall an esports organization: their League of Legends (LoL) team had been relegated, meaning it was demoted from the top tier of play, in the League of Legends Championship Series. At that time, the LCS was by far the most successful esports league in the world, due primarily to LoL's enormous player base: 100 million monthly players. When NRG was relegated, three months before BlizzCon, an LCS slot was estimated to be worth $1 million. It was as if the Boston Red Sox were told to leave the MLB and that they could play in the Minor Leagues if they desired to continue, a blow that would seem impossible for any team to recover from.

Now that NRG finally got its seat at Bobby's table, it

was vital that they managed to cut a deal. They assumed they were around the sixth or seventh organization that had been brought in for a one-on-one meeting and knew they were playing catch-up. Andy, Mark, Jeff, and Brett were expecting bad news about the availability of teams. They knew that teams were going to be based in a particular geographical region, similar to a traditional sports league, and they doubted that their preferred market, San Francisco, would still be available. "I thought Bobby was going to try to sell it to the Warriors or the 49ers or the Giants," said Andy. "I knew that all of them had come in because I'd talked to all of them about partnering with us. And they're all like, yeah, we're going to go in by ourselves to try and look at this." The issue was that San Francisco made far more sense than anywhere else as the choice home for NRG's team for a couple of reasons. Not only was it most convenient, with Andy and Mark both living in the region, but more importantly the Bay Area was one of the largest media markets in the United States with a high saturation of gamers. It was arguably the third-most-desirable US *Overwatch* market behind New York and Los Angeles.

Though the factors that influenced NRG's desired city were primarily financial in nature—in which market would NRG's owners stand the best chance of making money on their investment?—the decision would have a profound effect on the kids who would one day be signed by the team. The kids currently playing *Overwatch* in their bedrooms with their friends had no idea that they would soon be paid as much as $150,000 a year to play the game professionally, far from home, in a city determined by a handful of adults in a boardroom. For one of these kids, Jay Won, the Seattle market would be an easy transition: he already lived there. At the time of this meeting, Jay was fifteen years old. Jay would go from an unknown kid playing video games in his bedroom in the suburbs of Seattle to competing for the league championship in front of 12,000 fans. By then he would be the best player in the world. But where would he live?

It's hard to say whether Andy, Mark, and Brett were more nervous about the local market or the purchase price. The rumored cost of entry for the Overwatch League was $8 million, roughly $7 million more than had ever been paid for a team in an esports league. Though esports had attracted huge audiences in Asian markets, American esports had yet to prove it could capture the attention of the television networks, advertisers, and endorsers who pour the big money into the most popular professional sports.

Finally, an hour and a half into the meeting—after the chitchat subsided, the representatives of Activision-Blizzard shared their vision for OWL, and the structure had been discussed—Bobby told them that they could flip over the first piece of paper in front of them.

On the other side: a map of the Seattle media market.

The Seattle market had some attractive features: high income, high concentration of *Overwatch* players, good private jet access. But it was half the size of the Bay Area, just 3.6 million in all. They tried not to show their disappointment.

Bobby explained the details of the media market: they would be able to sell their own local broadcasting deals, they could own their own stadium, they could sell team sponsorships so long as they didn't conflict with league sponsorships, and so on. As Mark and Jeff engaged with Bobby, asking pointed questions about team rights and the expected level of league support in local markets, Andy remained silent. Brett knew he was disappointed. It wasn't just that San Francisco was a bigger market and that Andy lived in the Bay Area; it was that Andy really *wanted* the San Francisco market. It just felt right. Although the Seattle market still made financial sense, it just wasn't San Francisco. Brett worried that the emotional letdown would be the undoing of this venture. He was disappointed, too, but he wasn't the one putting up the money.

After walking them through the vision for their local market, Bobby scanned each of their faces. "Are you ready?" he asked. They nodded slowly, confused. "Okay,"

Bobby said. "Now you can turn over the second piece of paper."

Brett flipped it over: a map of the Bay Area.

That's when Bobby dropped the bomb on them: the purchase price would be $20 million.

CHAPTER 2

WHAT WAS ROBERT KRAFT THINKING?

What sort of lunatic would pay $20 million for a slot in an esports league? Robert Kraft was one such lunatic. He's best known for owning the New England Patriots, the team that's dominated the NFL since coach Bill Belichick and star quarterback Tom Brady came on board, winning six of the past eighteen Super Bowls. Kraft was also the first person to agree to become an owner in the Overwatch League, buying the Boston team.

How had Blizzard landed a whale like Robert Kraft? Probably over a beer after a round of golf, as Kraft and Bobby Kotick were friends. The Krafts were longtime investors in Activision-Blizzard, and when the two Bobs met at an investor conference in 2013, they quickly hit it off. But a businessman and sports empire builder like Kraft doesn't ink business deals to become friends (Exhibit A: employing Bill Belichick). There had to be financial sense somewhere in here.

Kraft was eager to get into OWL because he saw that the future of spectator sports was changing, and he wasn't going to let his empire be left behind. "We try to think long-term with everything we do," he explained, speaking of his organization. He said that they saw that the millennials and Gen Z were "consuming things differently," playing games hours and hours a day and not watching sports the way Kraft and his contemporaries did. "So we wanted to go with the best and try to participate in this whole new field," he said. "What I like about it more than anything is that it's a way to connect globally." There were, it seemed, three key components to his rationale for paying $20 million for the Boston franchise: it was what the young kids were doing, Bobby Kotick was "the best," and it would lead to global domination.

When Kraft said that the young kids "were consuming things differently" he meant that they didn't pay for cable television, which had typically been the moneymaker for professional sports. Besides the eleven games a season available to Amazon Prime members, watching an NFL game required a cable or satellite subscription, which only approximately 60 percent of millennials had. (A fifth had cut the cord, while the remaining fifth never signed up in the first place.) Even worse, the proportion that did have paid TV subscriptions appeared to be shrinking. That left Kraft with nothing to offer a huge portion of young Bostonians who wanted to show support for their city.

Esports was one of the places these elusive millennials seemed to be spending the time they saved by snubbing the NFL. While less than 5 percent of Americans aged thirteen to seventeen had watched an NFL game, 16 percent had watched esports. The growth issue went further than cable subscriptions: the average age of an NFL fan was in the midfifties, and that average age had been increasing every year—as the old fans died off, they weren't being replaced by young fans following the game anywhere, whether in person at stadiums, on TV, or even in highlight clips online. NFL ratings took their most dramatic dive in decades in the 2016 and 2017 seasons, with ratings down 8 percent in 2016 and another 9 percent in 2017. For those with billions of dollars tied up in NFL-related assets, that was an alarming decline, which created a good climate to attract NFL owners to an esports league.

Although esports were loaded with exactly the young people that the Kraft Group needed—the average age of an esports fan is twenty-four—the decision to dive in was not made easy by the fact that in the years before OWL, it had been a terrible place to invest. Nobody had been able to replicate the holy trinity of league design, advertiser sponsorship, and broadcasting rights that underpins the success of traditional sports leagues. Without those three elements providing structure, reliable revenue, and a way to connect with the fans, team owners couldn't make money. As a result, esports leagues had been marred by chaos. Teams disbanded midseason because management couldn't make payroll, while other teams disintegrated because the players didn't get along (and, presumably, there wasn't enough money coming in to force them to play nice), while others disappeared for no apparent reason. The popularity of different video games ebbed and flowed, and players jumped ship accordingly. To add to this chaos, the biggest esports leagues used a relegation model in which the worst-performing teams each year were sent down to a lower-tier league, effectively disappearing, which made owners and potential owners reluctant to invest big money in a team whose value, depending on its performance, could evaporate overnight.

Even the young audience that traditional sports owners needed to find a way to capture were something of a long-term investment, a double-edged sword from an advertising perspective. TV networks such as CBS, NBC, Fox, and ESPN paid billions of dollars for distribution rights for traditional sports so that they could sell advertising—the commercial spots that go along with games, the real estate on the screen during gameplay where various logos are jammed, and whatever other kinds of sponsorships they could come up with. The challenge of courting young audiences was that although they represented a lucrative *future* for distribution networks (assuming the fans continued to watch esports when they entered the workforce and their incomes grew), they weren't a lucrative audience for advertisers at present. Advertisers paid money for access to people with disposable income—the richer the viewers, the more they would pay—and today's esports fans weren't worth much, at least not yet.

I spoke to an investor who considered purchasing an OWL team but ultimately couldn't get comfortable. The way he looked at the investment, a traditional sports fan could bring in about $54 per year. (He arrived at this number by adding up all the revenues of the major traditional sports and dividing by the number of fans.) For esports, these numbers were $800 million in revenues per year, and 400 million fans, which made each fan worth $2 per year, one-twenty-seventh of the value of a traditional sports fan. Why were those values so different? Primarily because their youth translated to low disposable income. But even beyond that, they had a generational problem: millennials, having come of age during the Great Recession, had lower lifetime incomes for their age than previous generations such as boomers. Beyond that, about half of esports fans were Chinese, and the average person in China earned just one-eighth of what the average American did. Finally, the vast majority of esports fans were men (or boys, as the case may be)—even more so than in traditional sports—and women more often determine how money gets spent on consumer products. (According to the *Harvard Business Review,* women control between 70 and 80 percent of consumer spending in the United States.) The only consumer categories where men make the decisions were power tools, lawn care, auto tires, and certain consumer electronics categories (e.g., gaming hardware). For these many reasons, most traditional advertisers had no interest in advertising to esports fans.

Assuming the league could crack the formula to get major advertisers aboard, there remained another major risk for owners: what some perceived as the toxicity of esports culture. As a form of entertainment embraced by teenage boys, video games have always had their share of immature traditions, some more harmful than others. Perhaps the best known of them is "tea bagging," a repeated squat that a player will do over the virtual body of a player they have killed (the "tea bag" is supposed to reference the scrotum, though that level of anatomy has thankfully not been rendered in any video game I'll admit to having seen). Blizzard was sensitive to this and knew that they needed to stamp out any notion that the culture was toxic as soon as it arrived. When one of the best-known players in the league said that an openly gay player on a rival team would probably like to "suck a fat c***," the company treated the entire league as if it had a homophobia problem. They had seen the NFL's mismanagement of domestic violence cases cause PR nightmares for advertisers, who wanted to avoid seeming complicit in silencing women abused by NFL players. Blizzard didn't want any sponsors or owners pondering a $20 million purchase to consider esports a risk—and any esports player getting attention for horrible behavior created that risk.

Beyond the culture, there was also the controversial violence of shooting games that made some owners uneasy. Video games have carried a stigma regarding violence ever since the Columbine High School shooting, where the perpetrators were gamers who played *Doom* and *Quake*. The families of the victims of Columbine blamed video games for the shooting and sued twenty-five video-game publishers for $5 billion, including the makers of *Quake* and *Doom*. One of the Columbine shooters allegedly named his shotgun Arlene, after the love interest of the main character in *Doom*. Although the suit was tossed out, the attention didn't dissipate. *Doom* was arguably the goriest game ever made at the time the tragedy of Columbine occurred in 1999, with demons exploding in fountains of blood and chainsaws used to saw enemies in half, rendered with disturbing, vivid detail. Despite the attention that Columbine drew to the potential effects of playing violent games—attention that has perennially returned—study after study has failed to establish any causal link. (The American Psychological Association found that studies attempting to make the link were too methodologically flawed to consider seriously.) But that didn't mean that the perception that video games caused violence didn't concern potential owners and sponsors. After all, it had already held video games back from the Olympics, whose president, Thomas Bach, had said of including video games as an event, "We cannot have in the Olympic program a game which is promoting violence." (He made no reference to boxing or fencing, the latter in which he had once competed at the Olympics and both of which remain events.)

Given all the risks, the powerful special interests aligned against video games, and the wastelands of investments that esports had sunk to date, why did Kraft, the owner of the NFL's premier team, have any interest in getting involved? What did other NFL owners like Stan Kroenke of the Los Angeles Rams, who would end up acquiring one of LA's Overwatch franchises, see in OWL? Whatever it was, the Wilpons—owners of the New York Mets, who would go on to buy the New York franchise—seemed to see the same thing. As did a co-owner of the MLB's Texas Rangers, who put the money up for OWL's Houston franchise; Andy Miller and Mark Mastrov, co-owners of the NBA's Sacramento Kings, who with another partner acquired the San Francisco franchise; and Comcast, which bought the Philadelphia franchise.

Assuming that Kotick and the team he put together for OWL could somehow figure out how to attract advertisers, there *was* a big reason for all these business tycoons to be excited about OWL: because Blizzard created the game and it owned all rights and intellectual property to it, they had immense bargaining power over the players. Unlike with traditional sports like football, where some version of the game had oftentimes been played for thousands of years and no one owned the intellectual property (imagine having the exclusive rights to the forward pass!), Blizzard owned everything about Overwatch, and so players who were unhappy with salaries across the league couldn't walk. In the NFL, players could in theory take their ball and go form their own league if the league wasn't paying enough. Every five years, when the players and owners negotiated a new NFL deal, that was exactly what the

CHAPTER 3

THE PERFECT ESPORTS LEAGUE

There was a time when the Overwatch League was one man: Nate Nanzer, commissioner. Before being tapped for that role, he'd already been at Blizzard for two years, first in analytics and then as head of Blizzard's esports efforts. (Pre-OWL, Blizzard had run professional leagues in four of their games—*Hearthstone, Heroes of the Storm, Starcraft II,* and *World of Warcraft Arena*—offering $2.2 million in tournament prizes total across all four games.) The first season of OWL was to operate on a scale like nothing Nate and Blizzard had done before—it would offer a $3.5 million prize pool. In addition to the bigger prize money, OWL would offer substantially more job security to its players.

The steady income helped attract the top players to the league, but it wasn't what had attracted the top gamers to *Overwatch* in the first place—that was a function of its acclaimed gameplay. Even before there were whispers of an official league, many of the best players had begun taking time from *League of Legends* leagues and other games that paid them to play Overwatch for fun—in fact, every single player who would make up the 114-person OWL in its first season had already been playing the game for six months by the time the league was announced. Bdosin, who would become the lead shot caller for the London Spitfire, was one of those players, perhaps one of the best dozen or so mid-laners in the world in LoL. We'd never know for sure, though, because he was signed to the team that employed Rookie, selected unanimously as #1 in the world in ESPN's 2018 LoL mid-lane power rankings. But even with a large talent pool interested in the game, Nate had enormous problems to solve: namely, how to design the league so that Blizzard would make money operating it, while still offering an attractive investment to team owners; how to attract a fan base and sponsors willing to pay to advertise to that fan base; and how to ensure the league sustained itself when so many other esports efforts had failed to live up to their promises.

Nate knew about industries going sideways, then rapidly downhill, having brought a tapestry of challenging experiences to Blizzard. Prior to joining the video-game publisher, he'd spent eight years as a consultant at Frank N. Magid Associates, a company that was once to newspapers what Nielsen was to television. It had followed newspapers over the cliff—or given that they were supposed to provide intelligence to newspapers, perhaps it was the papers following *them*. Before Magid, Nate had spent eight years working for Penn, Schoen, and Berland Associates, the firm cofounded by Mark Penn, the well-known political pollster who discovered the "soccer moms" who helped reelect Bill Clinton. Both jobs required a rare combination of an analytical mind and a sense of polish, even a taste for performance. It was perfect training for his primary task in setting up OWL, which was crunching the numbers to determine how everyone was going to make money, then presenting that vision to the wealthiest sports owners in the world. (Then he would need to crunch a whole new set of numbers related to viewership, engagement, and strange metrics like "brand activations" to convince companies like T-Mobile that sponsoring OWL was a good idea.)

Before any of that, though, he had to answer a fundamental question about league design, and his answer would have a substantial impact on the type of owners he would be able to attract to the league. Nate would have to decide whether to follow a relegation model, similar to major esports leagues and European soccer leagues, or a franchise model, the one adopted by every American sports league. It was not a trivial decision. Although a franchise model would protect the value of the teams (and thus make them not only more valuable but easier to sell), it could hurt the value of distribution and sponsorship, because those partners might be concerned about the level of competition in the league.

At the time, the LoL Championship Series was considering switching from the relegation model to the franchise model. On the one hand, the relegation model, in addition to allowing for rags-to-riches stories, would improve the level of competition, because a perennial poor performer would be bumped from the top league to lower development leagues, rather than continuing to rake in millions in revenue as the worst part of a successful league, like the Cleveland Browns in the NFL. The LCS were wondering whether anyone wanted to be a fan for a league where those wealthy enough to afford a team could stay and profit even if they weren't competent enough to win.

On the other hand, Major League Soccer (MLS) saw the risks of relegation for owners, and in 2017 they rejected a $4 billion distribution deal, in large part because it required the MLS to adopt a relegation model instead of the current franchise model, even though the deal would have more than quadrupled the MLS's annual media revenues, from $90 million to $400 million per year.

Nate decided that despite the benefits, the relegation model wasn't worth the challenge it would present for owners. A franchise model was the way to go. It came down to the type of owner he wanted to attract to the league. Nate knew that guys like Jack Etienne who loved esports would want to be involved no matter how Nate set it up, so he needed to cater to the billionaire sports team owners he otherwise would struggle to get involved. Those owners were looking to grow major assets by owning a team, and the year-to-year profitability wasn't terribly important. (In fact, many NFL teams were run at a loss, which is fine if you have millions of dollars of other income, as the losses shield taxes on other gains.) Nate knew that the quickest way to lose a billionaire's interest in owning an OWL team would be floating the idea that if he didn't pay close enough attention, the team could slip through a hole in the bottom of the league, losing over 90 percent of its value.

So Nate made an atypical decision about esports league design, one that borrowed from traditional sports: franchises would be city based. Right up until the launch of the Overwatch League, esports was much more of an international scene than an American one. In all of the key video-game titles that had driven the esports scene pre-OWL—*Counter-Strike*, *League of Legends*, and *Dota 2*—there were far more fans in countries like South Korea, China, and Brazil than in the United States, and competitive players had to constantly travel around the world, with the championships often changing locations every year. Given that a team of pros might live in multiple countries and simply convene in whatever city the next tournament was in, the idea of local teams never developed. Nate's vision for the Overwatch League was different, a local-global hybrid: teams based in particular cities, competing in one game, in one league that spanned the globe. It would for the first time in esports localize fan bases, hoping to put them into contact with each other—at live games certainly but also walking down the street, where you might see someone in your local city's jersey—and in doing so create a virtual cycle of buzz and free marketing.

Before the Overwatch League launched, only one league had ever attempted a franchise model with city-based teams, and it had been the biggest financial disaster in esports history. The Championship Gaming Series, created in 2006, made many strange decisions. Each team competed in four different games: *Counter-Strike, Dead or Alive*

4 (a fighting game), *FIFA '07* (soccer), and a racing game. If you cared about your local team but you didn't like watching one of those games, that was too bad for you: your fortunes would be tied to it anyway. The league had also suffered from the fact that video-game graphics were not particularly good back then, and the games looked pixilated and jerky, appearing even more so when juxtaposed to shots of the broadcasters or the players. Some of the production touches, such as the in-game digital basketball jerseys that were superimposed over the military uniforms of the players in *Counter-Strike*, looked ridiculous—and not in a good way. The league did manage to land the most famous esports pro at that time, Fatal1ty, as an announcer. They paid him $300,000 per year, but somehow his *Quake III* gaming skills did not translate to *Counter-Strike* commentary. The league draft was held at the Playboy Mansion in 2007, a decision that has not aged well. Instead of the planned $50 million investment over five years, that league was canceled after the second season.

The failure of the Championship Gaming Series would hang over the esports world for years. People debated the moral of its failure, with some such as Brett, president of NRG Esports, suggesting it was due to "horrible mismanagement at the top levels" and others suggesting video games would just never be viable as a spectator sport. If this second-ever attempt to start a major esports league failed, it seemed the second narrative would prevail. It could chill the flow of money into esports for decades.

Though Nate had settled on the franchise model, he still needed help figuring out how to avoid the missteps that had sunk the Championship Gaming Series. The first person Nate hired was a man named Christopher Mykles, better known as MonteCristo, probably the person most knowledgeable about esports on the planet. MonteCristo's role would be to determine who from the esports world should produce the first season of Overwatch, help recruit them, and provide the esports hand on the tiller during production meetings. He was a good pick for that, having worn nearly every hat in esports: journalist, publisher, tournament organizer, analyst, team owner, and now broadcaster. In addition to consulting on the development of OWL, he would be an analyst and broadcaster during the first season (in esports, broadcasters are actually called "shoutcasters," or more often just "casters"). Before Nate talked him into joining, Monte was at the very peak of esports production: broadcasting the biggest esport, LoL, for the biggest esports network, OGN, in the global heart of esports, Seoul. When I asked one of Monte's friends whether he was worried about Monte leaving that behind, he said, "No, not at all. Monte accomplishes everything he sets his mind to."

CHAPTER 4

THE MAKING OF A PRO GAMER

At the age of sixteen, Jay Won dropped out of high school in Seattle and moved to Atlanta to pursue a career playing video games. Jay had settled on the name Sinatraa to represent himself online. He was a fan of the rapper Logic, whose fourth mixtape was titled *Young Sinatra: Welcome to Forever*. Jay added the extra *a* because "Sinatra" was already taken. He thought so anyway. When I spoke with him about it he wasn't sure—perhaps he had just added the extra *a* for no reason at all. That is a pattern among video-game pros—they selected their names mostly on a whim, and the details were hazy.

At the point that Jay Won arrived in Atlanta, it was fair to say that his life as Jay ended and the life of Sinatraa began. By the time I met him, about a year later, he was one of the most famous *Overwatch* players in the world, with high expectations. He was on a guaranteed $150,000 one-year contract to play in OWL, which included free housing, health care, and half of the tournament winnings. It was a far cry from his start in Atlanta, where his first pro team, Selfless Gaming, provided free housing, "usually" a few meals a day, and $1,500 per month. Sinatraa's $150,000 OWL contract was the only one publicly known in the entire Overwatch League. That had benefits, like increasing the number of subscribers to his Twitch stream, but also afforded endless opportunities for shit talking when his lesser-paid teammates killed him in scrimmages.

Still, Sinatraa never regretted dropping out of school. "I h-a-a-a-a-ted it," he told me, stretching the word out to make his position unmistakable. Sinatraa was quiet, and among all the players that I interviewed, he was by far the most reticent and careful about his answers. School seemed to have struck a nerve, though, and he warmed to the subject a bit. "The only class I liked," he said, "was maybe PE. The one I hated the most was definitely either Spanish or chemistry. It's just, holy shit, it's so boring. It's just lectures every day. I'm just sleeping every day." What about how science explains the fabric of reality, leading humans to the very insights necessary to build video games? "Yeah if you actually care it's interesting," he conceded. "But I actually didn't care at all."

Though his parents had assumed throughout his high school years that Sinatraa was headed to college, he already knew college wasn't for him. "I had no clue what I was going to do besides video games," he confessed. "I didn't have a plan B." According to Andy, the cofounder of NRG who would sign the check on Sinatraa's $150,000 contract, his dad had hoped that Sinatraa would work with him in what Andy described as his "motorcycle chop shop." But Sinatraa was perplexed by that analysis. "Andy said that?" he asked me, his nose crinkling, eyes in a skeptical squint. The players had a lot of respect for Andy, and most of them in fact liked him, but they were still teenage kids. Their default assumption was that adults are bozos. "I have no idea what he's referring to," Sinatraa added. "I've never heard of that actually in my life." When I asked him what his father did for a living, he told me that "he's a technician type person. He takes apart and then resells. Stuff like that."

When Sinatraa arrived at the Selfless team house in Dunwoody, a suburb of Atlanta filled with four-bedroom houses with big lawns, he was nervous. He would be living in a house with strangers much older than he was. His five teammates ranged in age from twenty-two to thirty-three. He would be the only person in the house not legally allowed to drink or smoke. "It was a big move," he acknowledged. "At first I was actually kind of scared, dropping out of school, moving across the country, not seeing my friends and family." So Sinatraa brought his mom. She was supportive of his desire to become a pro gamer; in fact, she'd been the deciding factor. When Sinatraa had gotten the offer from Selfless the week before Christmas, he shared it with his mom, who said she was fine with it, but he couldn't bring himself to tell his dad. "I knew he would be skeptical," Sinatraa said. "On Christmas, we were having dinner, and it came out. Me, my brother, and my mom were trying to convince my dad that I should go. It was my mom mostly. She just kept saying it was my passion and what I wanted to do. We should just let him do what he wants." It worked.

Though she'd convinced her husband that Jay should drop out of high school and move across the country, Sinatraa's mom still wanted to meet the people she'd be turning her son over to.

It would be hard to find someone better designed to put a mother at ease than Daniel Martinez Paz, better known as Dhak. Eleven years older than Sinatraa, Dhak had already experienced enough to fill a lifetime when he joined Selfless. No two players had more dissimilar paths to OWL than he and Sinatraa, yet they would become not only teammates and roommates but close friends. They played opposite roles on the team. Sinatraa played the damage role, meaning he played heroes capable of dealing lots of damage to opponents, while Dhak played the support role, primarily a character called Lucio. Lucio, a Brazilian DJ on rollerblades, served two primary functions: he could speed up the movement of nearby teammates or heal them. A good Lucio player—and Dhak was one of the best in the world—will speed his team into a good combat position, then switch over to healing to keep them alive. It was a role that relied on paying very close attention to your teammates, and Dhak showed the same skill in person that made him such a talented Lucio in Overwatch. When you talked to him, he'd listen to everything you said, right to the end of the sentence, an exceedingly rare trait among the fast-twitch types who populated esports.

By the time Dhak arrived in Atlanta, he'd lived in Venezuela, Spain, the United Kingdom, and the United States. Those weren't just vacations: during his twenty-six years on earth, he'd spent at least three years in each of these countries. He spent the first twelve years of his life in a city in Venezuela called Maracay, population 1 million, situated on a lake about a two-hour drive from the capital, Caracas.

Dhak was born in Venezuela to Spanish parents, who had come to South America at different points in their lives, his mom as a child and his dad in his twenties, when Spain was suffering from an economic slump and Venezuela was up and coming. It was the 1970s, and Venezuela was the richest country in South America, while Spain was suffering from the same oil crisis that rocked the United States. Dhak didn't stay there longer because Hugo Chávez came into power, and his parents thought, "This guy is kind of crazy." Because his family had the means to go back to Spain, they did.

He was relieved by the safety of his new home. "In Venezuela it was like 'Where are you going? What time are you coming back?'" Dhak told me. "My parents had to be careful with what I did, and even I could feel the danger. In Spain I could be out at 3 a.m. on the streets and I'd be fine." If Dhak's parents hadn't decided to leave Venezuela, or hadn't been able to get out, then a multitude of darker Dhak time lines could be imagined. How many of them would have led him to the Overwatch League?

Dhak had already discovered his passion for gaming when he was in Venezuela, and his primary concerns about living there tended to be more gamer-centric than safety related. His chief concern was that he had to play on LAN, a local area network that functions offline, because the internet connection was not good enough for anything else. When he wanted to play multiplayer games, he would need to trudge over to the LAN café and play against whoever happened to be next to him. Dhak had started playing video games when he was two years old. Beginning with Atari, his dad purchased every console for his kids, and eventually Dhak's uncle, a "PC geek from early on," set up a PC in Dhak's bedroom. His uncle would occasionally come by to use it, but whenever he was gone, Dhak used it to play video games. Dhak discovered a PC game called *Age of Empires*, in the real-time strategy genre. He got hooked on that one, because its turn-based gameplay made it the rare game that even in Venezuela he could play online. (The lag in non-turn-based games—and how that affects a player's ability to respond to the action—are what make most games difficult to play without a strong internet connection.) Even at nine years old, he would play *Age of Empires* through the night, seeing the sun rise from his bed.

He quickly realized just how much he loved competing against others online—how it was the combination of the gameplay *with* the excitement of another human on the other end that hooked him. "I hate single-player games with a passion," he explained. "If I'm not playing against another person, I'm not interested. I know the computer has a pattern, and if I just learn it, it's not gonna adapt to what I'm doing. If I'm playing against a human being, he has a pattern, too, but he can change the pattern at any time. *That's* what's interesting." Though he was certainly right about the thrilling suspense of live gaming, it is also what can be devastating about player-versus-player gaming, particularly for fragile male egos attached to mediocre gaming skills. Player-versus-player games usually require high skill, the enjoyment of competition regardless of the result, or a case of masochism.

The move from Venezuela to Spain would change many aspects of Dhak's life, but it would not affect his ability to play *Counter-Strike* at LAN cafés. Dhak moved from the fifth-biggest city in Venezuela to the twentieth-biggest city in Spain, a town called Gijón on the Bay of Biscay, the body of water separating the north coast of Spain from the west coast of France. For his first year in Gijón, Dhak put video games aside. "Playing games is fun but I don't want to be friendless," he said. "I would go to basketball, and I met some friends there. Then one time I said, 'Yo, maybe you guys want to go to a LAN café and we can play video games.'" The experiment with games in real life didn't last long, as Dhak proceeded to spend the rest of his high school years playing CS with people he met in Gijón.

Dhak's first CS tournament was as eye-opening as his first visit to a LAN café. He was fourteen years old, meaning Sinatraa had just finished potty training. The tournament took place in Bilbao, about a three-hour drive east along the coast. On the way, he would pass by La Cueva del Castillo, which contains the oldest cave painting in the world, El Panel de las Manos. Dhak passed right by it without giving it a thought. The action for Dhak was in Bilbao, online. "My first big tournament I literally played against the best CS team in the world," he told me. "I played against SK. The prize pool for that LAN event was huge, €10,000. So it was worth it for teams in pretty much every city in Europe to travel to Bilbao to take a shot at winning. That's when I first saw pro players in person." Whereas Dhak and his friends had driven a few hours to get there, the professionals had arrived on a plane, carrying all sorts of swag from their sponsors. "They were on another level," Dhak confessed. His team got walloped, and for weeks afterward he couldn't stop thinking about the odd crew of guys who had rolled into town and taken home the prize money.

Dhak's eyes were opened to the prospect of becoming an esports pro, but he didn't make it his career goal just yet. He continued going to school, expecting to go to college to keep his career options open. By the time Dhak needed to take the college entrance exam a couple of years later, he was playing CS for eleven hours a day on weekdays and close to forty hours over the weekend—ninety-five hours a week in all—while maintaining a B+ average at school.

Dhak figured he ought to devote just enough energy to his classes to ensure that he would pass the university entrance exam. "I knew I needed at least a 4.2," he told me, to keep "80 percent of careers open to me." And, because he believed he could hit that threshold without studying, he avoided it entirely, trying to optimize his time and by scoring exactly a 4.2. Which is what he did, 4.2 on the dot, with not a single extraneous second spent on studying.

If esports had been something he could have pursued in college, then Dhak might have gone to college. Today, more than twenty colleges in the United States have varsity esports teams, and fifteen of those colleges offer scholarships to players, with the latest to join being the sports powerhouse the Ohio State University. But at the time Dhak was considering college, none of those programs existed.

Unsure what he wanted to throw himself into, Dhak decided to take a yearlong sabbatical and study English in San Diego, California. While he prepared to move to the United States, Sinatraa was discovering his first love.

The game that first hooked Sinatraa was called *Jak and Daxter*, a player-versus-environment game, the kind that Dhak hated. Sinatraa described being nine or ten years old when he started playing *Jak and Daxter* with his older brother. Sinatraa soon moved on to the types of games Dhak favored: first-person-shooters. "The next game I loved was *Halo 3*." Sinatraa paused. This would happen many more times, whenever pro players were reminded of playing *Halo 3*, their minds pulling them back to the intricate maps and favorite weapons, the close games of capture the flag, all their online gamer teammates they'd spent hundreds of hours playing *Halo 3* with and then never spoken to again. I came to think of it as the *Halo 3* pause, a flash of memory of the halcyon times when gaming was still a culturally ignored, mildly embarrassing hobby. Before the hundred-thousand-dollar contracts, before the media spotlight, before anyone had even heard the word "toxicity." Nope, it wasn't any of that. *Halo 3* just ruled. After listening to Sinatraa list the titles of the other games he loved that would eventually lead him to *Overwatch*, it became clear that his time line didn't add up. There was simply no way he could have been nine or ten when he played *Jak and Daxter. Jak and Daxter* came out just before Sinatraa's first birthday, and by seven years old he was already playing *Halo 3*. Sinatraa had been a dedicated gamer since before he could remember.

Sinatraa first realized that gaming could earn him money, albeit only a paltry sum at that point, when he started playing *Call of Duty: Modern Warfare 2*. His approach to that game was to focus on trick shooting: he would camp out in different nooks on the maps until an enemy unwittingly crept close, then ambush the enemy with an unlikely stunt in which he jumped from above and used a sniper rifle to kill him point-blank with a single headshot. He had others record videos of him doing this and put them on YouTube, where he could earn money off ad revenue.

Who thinks that is a good way to spend time? Nine-year-olds do, and, when *Call of Duty: Modern Warfare 2* was released, Sinatraa was nine. How much money did he make doing this? "I didn't make much," Sinatraa told me sheepishly. I tossed out a lowball guess, fifty dollars a month? "Bro, not even that much." He laughed as he said it, but he still seemed embarrassed that at nine years old he was making less than fifty dollars a month playing video games. This seemed odd. It's possible he had lingering embarrassment about his plans to make a career of playing video games, perhaps remembering all the eye rolls in the decade before he signed a $150,000 contract. More likely, though, the same thing that drove Sinatraa to be so fiercely competitive playing video games also drove him toward more typical American goals, such as making money. Despite saying that he had no plan B, if Sinatraa had been born forty years earlier, in 1960, I imagine him at a bond-trading desk at Salomon Brothers surrounded by rotary phones. Watching the speed and coordination with which he manipulated a dozen phones, connecting buyers with sellers at an inhuman rate, his colleagues would probably bestow upon him the same nickname he would earn from his Overwatch League teammates: the alien.

A little more than a thousand miles south of Seattle, Dhak was also learning how to monetize gaming. While attending his English courses in San Diego, he had only a laptop, and, because it wasn't powerful enough to play CS, he had to find a different game. He started playing online poker, and soon he was spending every waking moment outside of class seeing hands. By the time his English course was over, he had already made $100,000 playing poker online. He moved back in with his family in Spain and earned another $200,000 playing poker for another year. Then when his brother went to college in Spain, Dhak decided he would join him. That lasted three months, until Spain passed a law that limited online gambling to only people within the country, so he decided he needed to leave.

He ended up moving to England, where gambling was tax-free, with four other poker players he had met online. "I didn't know them in person," Dhak confessed, "but from my experience in gaming I knew that you get better when you play next to other people. These CS pros from Sweden," he said, referencing the team that wiped the floor in the first competitive tournament he had entered, "I knew they were better because they had a better LAN café. When you're playing something and you're sitting next to the other guy, and you see how he holds his keyboard, and you can ask, 'Why did you do that?' Because of that

I knew that living with other poker players would make me a better poker player." So he moved to England for a couple of years.

While Dhak settled into life as a professional poker player, Sinatraa became consumed with *Call of Duty: Black Ops 2*, which turned him on to a website called Gamebattles. Gamebattles offered a way for extremely serious players like Sinatraa to face off against a chosen team of other serious players, but the way it integrated—or more accurately failed to integrate—with the games themselves was puzzling. Any modern online multiplayer game, including *Overwatch* and every *Call of Duty* release, has a built-in multiplayer mode. In more recent iterations, players can ascend in rank and play against better players (instead of being randomly tossed into whichever match started next). But that's not enough for the most intense gamers. Gamebattles allowed players to register their team on the website and then challenge other teams to a match. Because the software wasn't integrated into the game, the winning team had to snap a picture of the result. Thus, the Gamebattles subreddit has been forever dominated by people complaining about not getting proper credit for a win (which affects ranking and real-money tournament qualification). For Sinatraa, Gamebattles was a brief dalliance, at eleven years old, on his way to bigger things, but the fact that it even exists showed that the supply side for competitive gaming has always been strong. In other words, there have been plenty of hypercompetitive gamers who want to prove they're the best, regardless of how imperfect the system they must work within. American gamers had been waiting for people like Bobby Kotick and Nate Nanzer, people who could build a sustainable competitive system to connect this eager supply with demand, viewers, and convince advertisers to pay for the whole thing. There had been dozens of attempts before OWL, but the only leagues with sustained success relied on Asian and European viewers. The United States remained the great white whale.

The final leg of Dhak's journey to Overwatch began in the United States, where he moved at the age of twenty-five to start college. His decision to move there was spontaneous. Dhak and his poker buddies had taken a monthlong vacation to Cancún. On the day they were set to return to England, Dhak packed his bags, but he never made it to the airport. "In Cancún it was warm. I could go to the pool, I could go to the beach. I realized I never wanted to go back to England again in my life." He told his friends they could keep or sell off his stuff, and he booked a flight to Miami. Dhak had believed the United States was likely to legalize online poker soon, and with his brother in Miami studying at Broward College, he decided to follow. He had plenty of money for college from his poker playing and knew that he liked cooking, so he enrolled in Broward's culinary arts program.

He didn't know what he was getting into. In the first year of the culinary arts program, his work involved only classes, which he found to be easy. The next year he had to go into the field and cook, which Dhak described as "the hardest thing I've ever done in my life." Up to that point, he said he'd had an easy life, playing poker and video games at home and pulling in more than enough money to cover his expenses. As a line cook, however, he had to be on his feet the whole day. He woke up at 5:00 a.m., cooked breakfast, then lunch, then dinner, and at the end of the day he would need to prep for the next day. When he got back home at 6:00 or 7:00 p.m., the last thing he wanted to do was play poker. Instead, he would do homework and then maybe one or two hours of *Counter-Strike*, which he found more entertaining (if much less lucrative) than his poker games. He kept on telling himself he could go back to poker once he finished college, but he knew he was falling behind the learning curve. He'd heard from his friends that games were getting tougher. But he was having too much fun playing CS to stop.

Then *Overwatch* was announced, and with its similarities to CS and advanced team gameplay, he knew it was one he wanted to try. "It looked fun," he said, shrugging. In less than two years, he'd earn more than $50,000 and become a household name for tens of millions of people in a game he started playing because it looked fun.

What do Sinatraa and Dhak teach us about how you become a pro gamer? Maniacal dedication is clearly necessary, which takes the form of 8 hours a day of gaming after going to school, plus the entirety of the weekend. That adds up to about 75 hours a week of gaming on top of 40 hours a week of school (total number of hours in a week: 168). But judging by Sinatraa and Dhak's path, even 75 hours of practice a week may not be enough—115 was what was required for them, which left about 7 ½ hours per day for dinner and sleep. The lifestyle of a pro gamer may seem like a lazy teenager's dream, but it is in fact extraordinarily rigorous, so demanding on one's time that it doesn't seem to have left space for any of the OWL players I've studied to have a girlfriend or play a sport. (Note: As this book went to press, nearly all of the pro gamers featured had girlfriends, most of whom they'd met online through their Twitch chat or from Twitter direct messages. Also, Danteh played soccer.)

To devote oneself so fully, one must of course *not* see this commitment as a sacrifice, and talking with Dhak and Sinatraa, that is certainly the sense you get. For all those hours every day, they've been doing something they loved,

CHAPTER 5

HOW BILLY BEANE WOULD
BUILD AN OVERWATCH TEAM

The first team that signed Dhak and Sinatraa, Selfless Gaming, was run by a man named Brad Rajani, the son of an African immigrant father and an American midwestern mother. Brad had dreams of being a pro gamer in his youth, but he was born in the wrong year, reaching the age of peak video-game ability before pro gaming was a viable career. He started online gaming in 1997, when he was thirteen, playing *Command and Conquer* and *Duke Nukem*. There was a competitive platform of sorts called Total Entertainment Network, which was sophisticated for its time. "They had an Elo system and everything," Brad told me, describing the system that weights the value of a victory by the difference in skill level of the players (e.g., beating someone much worse than you hardly boosts your ranking).

There was a *Command and Conquer: Red Alert* and *Quake* championship in an upstart league called Professional Gamers League the next year, which Brad attended, hosted in an unglamorous store called Gameworks. At the age of fourteen, Brad took third place in *Command and Conquer*, receiving $7,500 and an AMD computer. The winner of the *Quake* tournament was Dennis Fong, better known as Thresh, recognized by Guinness World Records as the first professional gamer, for whom the computer and $7,500 could hardly compare to his prior tournament prize, a Ferrari 328. And not just any Ferrari 328 but the personal Ferrari of John Carmack, cofounder and technical director of id Software (creators of *Quake, Doom,* and *Wolfenstein 3D*) and who would later become CTO of Oculus VR, the virtual reality technology company that Facebook bought in 2014 for $2 billion.

Though Brad was around for these origins of professional esports, it is fair to say that for most of his peak playing years it was seen as more of a hobbyist endeavor. Sure, Thresh managed to make a good go of it, earning $250,000 from 1997 to 1999 including tournament winnings, sponsorships, and book royalties—roughly $83,000 per year—but he was in a league of his own. Nobody would come close to that money in esports until Johnathan Wendel, better known as Fatal1ty, came on the scene in 1999 playing *Quake III* and, during an eight-year career, raked in a total of $450,000 from tournament winnings alone, roughly $56,000 per year. Like Thresh, he was in a league of his own. Over the course of the pro gaming careers of first Thresh and then Fatal1ty, the first ten years of esports, only one US pro earned more than $50,000 per year. In the inaugural season of OWL, $50,000 was the minimum that more than a hundred players would make.

The way Brad saw it, there was a whole generation of professional esports players who lived off of slim tournament prizes, not salaried but putting in full-time effort, surviving off meager winnings and only able to attend the tournaments in the first place because they covered airfare for finalists. He knew about this lost generation of gamers because he was a member of it.

With the sudden influx of money into the industry with the launch of OWL, Brad could theoretically have made a go at being a professional again, but he knew that the odds were weighted heavily against him. "The gaming population has grown so much," he explained. "The odds of being amazing among this much bigger of a group is that much harder." Perhaps even more significant for Brad and his cohorts in esports' lost generation, reaction times start to decline in the early twenties, perhaps even earlier, and one's growing responsibilities can make staying competitive difficult. "You get a family and a job," Brad says, "and it's very difficult to play against a high schooler who can play ten hours a day after school."

From Fatal1ty's retirement in 2006 to the launch of *Overwatch* in 2016, many American esports leagues came, and nearly just as many went. Much of the reason is that almost every successful esports league launched since the early days was managed by the company that created the game, and as soon as game sales decline to a low enough threshold, they see little reason to continue funding the league. The one exception to that structure was ELEAGUE, the *Counter-Strike: Global Offensive* (CS: GO) league that Brett actually helped launch in 2015. That league broadcast its fourth season on TBS in 2019. Providing a high level of competition for a beloved game, ELEAGUE was an instant hit, and since its start four years before, it had added two games: *Street Fighter* and *Rocket League*. ELEAGUE was also the catalyst for Brad to form Selfless Gaming and therefore the reason that he came back to esports. He'd been away from it for fifteen years to go to college and join his family's behavioral health-care services business, where he had risen to director of finance and oversaw a team of a dozen people. He saw that the United States was ready for esports like it never had been, and this time he wasn't going to let anything stop him from getting a piece of that pie. But it would not be easy to explain to his father, an immigrant who had fled an oppressive dictator to chase the opportunity the United States provided him as an entrepreneur, why he planned to leave the company without a head of finance.

Brad started Selfless Gaming with about $100,000 and a plan to build a CS: GO roster for ELEAGUE. Soon after starting Selfless, *Overwatch* came out, and Brad decided he wanted to build a team there, too.

Although everyone told Brad not to look to *Overwatch*'s in-game ranking system—"the Ladder"—for recruitment prospects, he was skeptical. The Ladder had come under attack because of legitimate problems. Most notably, your ranking determined whom you would get paired with in games, and getting paired with teammates much worse than you in games so heavily reliant on teamwork is a frustrating experience, so people initially tried to game it. The problem was that scoring individual feats such as "kills" could help a player's rank even if they're strategically damaging to their team: the team could lose, but the rogue killer could move up the Ladder. After observing this unintended consequence, Blizzard removed individual skill as a component of Ladder rankings. This created new issues—for instance, top players banding together to ensure wins—requiring further fine-tuning. This is part and parcel of modern competitive gaming: no system arrives perfectly designed, and gamers are going to figure out how to exploit it. That's just how they're wired. Still, Brad managed to find value in the ever-changing Ladder, and he moved away from the safe approach used by other teams: signing pro players who'd been cut from their teams in other FPS games, like CS: GO and *Call of Duty.*

Brad didn't want a team that would just be competitive; he wanted to beat the Overwatch teams of the big-money sports organizations those players were getting cut from. He looked to the Ladder, thinking that the criticisms of it "smacked of hubris," of "the rationalizations that players go through to try to explain their position in the world." But he didn't just look at who was at the top of the Ladder and approach them; he dove deep into the stats—accuracy percentages, kill/death ratios, time spent on fire, damage numbers—looking for indicators that a player wasn't just a rogue stat compiler but an active team participant with superior skill.

That is how Brad found Dafran, whom many consider the best *Overwatch* player in the world at tracking (tracking is the ability to maintain your crosshairs on an enemy, preferably on their head, while they try to avoid being shot by you). "His accuracy percentage was a standard deviation above everyone else," Brad said.

But Dafran's story wasn't one of quick and easy successes, and when Brad told me one day that, in forming a team, he has always "preferred the approach of harnessing the power of the gods, so to speak, of finding the players that have talent and try to work with them, instead of taking the less talented, more coachable ones," I knew that he had Dafran in mind. During his time playing for Brad on Selfless, Dafran would be permanently banned from professional *Overwatch*.

But that would be months away. Soon after signing Dafran, Selfless invited Sinatraa to an online tryout. He'd caught their eye by hitting rank #2 in North America and fifth in the world on the Ladder. In a tryout, prospects are mixed with players already on the team so that coaches can observe how they communicate and work together. Sinatraa played well, but Selfless cut him loose anyway. Sinatraa said that he didn't make the team "because of a certain player" (Sinatraa refused to name the player, having learned diplomacy since becoming a highly paid *Overwatch* pro). The issue was that Sinatraa and this mystery player both played the damage role, specifically Tracer, the flagship hero of *Overwatch*, and Sinatraa had destroyed him in the tryout.

Tracer is a British tart in a jumpsuit who dual-wields laser pistols. According to Blizzard, she's a lesbian. Her special abilities allow her to move forward or backward in time. This makes her extremely mobile. Her pistols do a lot of damage, especially when aimed at the head, so when she gets up close to an enemy hero with a low maximum amount of health—what gamers call a "squishy" hero— they usually die. Seeing Tracer suddenly "blink" out of thin air in front of you is the stuff of *Overwatch* nightmares, and when you see it happen to a professional player, especially if they play a squishy, immobile hero (e.g., Zenyatta), you can see on their face the image of pure panic, followed almost immediately by resignation. Watching that happen to these teenagers is in fact the only time that I felt like I had something in common with them, because it's exactly what I encountered every time I tried to play with them: upon encountering an enemy, I panicked and died.

Tracer was a particularly challenging hero to master because of her abilities and the role she played for her team. Tracer's job was either to flank the opposing team, bringing in damage from an unexpected direction, or to hunt down the opposing team's healers or snipers hiding behind the battle. This made Tracer play a solitary endeavor: Sinatraa had to rely entirely on his own wits and skill to accomplish his mission. Owing to the high mobility afforded by her unique abilities, playing

Tracer required even more extreme reflexes than other heroes, which is a tall order. Every professional *Overwatch* player—whether they perform a support role such as healing their teammates or a tank role that soaks up damage and creates space for the team—had incredible reflexes. The game moved so blindingly fast that the most typical comment I heard from the various dads chaperoning their young sons across the country to watch a match in Los Angeles was, "I have no idea what's going on." These were my sentiments exactly early in the season, and though I eventually adjusted to the pace of the game, I was certain that I would never be able to follow Sinatraa's Tracer play. It was just too fast.

The situation between Sinatraa and the other Tracer on Selfless had grown tense in the tryout because it was clear that Sinatraa was the best Tracer outside South Korea. If he joined the team, he would take the one spot for Tracer in the starting lineup. So the guy already on the team blackballed him, claiming he was toxic.

Despite this, a few weeks later, Selfless invited Sinatraa to another tryout. He was just too good to resist a second look. This time Brad was watching, and after the first game, he turned to his assistant coach and said, "That is the best Tracer play I've ever seen." They signed him immediately, and sure enough, the player who blackballed him was sent packing. Brad sold him to another team.

This would be Brad's pattern. Brad had established a system of scouting players from the Ladder, signing them for $1,500 a month, and then selling them for tens of thousands of dollars once they'd popped off in a tournament. Just as Billy Beane had famously sold off his closers in *Moneyball*, Brad traded away talented players knowing he could always scout another unsigned one on the Ladder. And once the dust settled on the first season of OWL, there would be good reason to believe Brad was the best *Overwatch* scout in the world.

Dhak had joined Brad's team three months before Sinatraa. He had become a standout *Overwatch* player early, realizing he had found his new passion before the game was even released: he managed to get his hands on a beta version of the game through a Blizzard employee he knew. He decided to go pro after his first all-night session.

Dhak had been picked primarily for his Lucio, an essential hero to any successful team since day one of *Overwatch*. The dominant compositions of teams were constantly changing, with the balances of power among the heroes shifting every time Blizzard tweaked the game, while a few times a year entirely new heroes were introduced, but Lucio maintained a permanent spot on winning rosters for the entire existence of Selfless Gaming, meaning Dhak's roster spot was locked.

As the cast of the game—and the power of each of

their abilities—shifted, so have the dominant strategies. For instance, in the inaugural season of the Overwatch League, a composition became prevalent called "dive," in which six highly mobile heroes work together to get to the high ground before "diving" off into the opposing team's back line, where the squishy support players are hiding. Of course, the dominance of the dive composition spawned counter-dive compositions, which necessitated new strategies or tactics, swapping out a hero based on the map or situation, and on and on. This push and pull of strategies within the current state of the game is referred to as "the meta," short for metagame. (The game of *Overwatch* involves achieving an objective, such as capturing territory, while killing your enemies and avoiding dying. The metagame of *Overwatch* involves using a particular composition of heroes, strategies, and tactics to achieve the objectives within the game.) The rest of *Overwatch* history has proceeded apace, with innovative approaches dominating the game to create a new meta, then becoming unseated by the next, as Blizzard tweaked the game to keep the hero powers and the different kinds of strategies in balance, inevitably surprised by the novel ways in which the best players in the world exploit their so carefully considered tweaks and necessitate new ones.

Like a government trying to optimize the welfare of its citizens, Blizzard's task was thankless, and Blizzard inevitably found themselves the target of fan, and occasionally even player, ire. After all, their decisions could hold sway over a player's entire career, instantly destroying the contributions they could offer a team with a simple update. For this reason, it was unwise for players to "one-trick," or master only one hero. At the highest level, mastering a hero requires extensive practice—not just to perfect the abilities of the hero but also to understand the subtleties of how that hero's role and responsibilities change given your team compositions *and* given every possible enemy team composition, on every part of every single map. The inaugural season of *Overwatch* included seventeen maps. To master a single hero at the professional level required an enormous time investment but wasn't enough for a sustainable career. The OWL audience could grow tired of seeing a hero as part of every team and complain to Blizzard, *Overwatch* lead designer Jeff Kaplan and the design team might just decide that one hero was simply too powerful and nerf—or make less potent, like a Nerf gun—it to oblivion, or a newly introduced hero could render a once-essential hero obsolete. There were any number of ways for a one-trick pro to become suddenly useless, all of them completely out of the player's control. Despite the trade-offs (spending time mastering a second or third hero compromises mastery of the first hero, especially given the ever-evolving meta), *Overwatch* pros have to maintain a diversified hero pool to sustain a career.

Sinatraa was eager to join Selfless, but there was an obstacle for him that Brad had never before faced: Sinatraa was still a minor, just sixteen years old. Brad didn't need to convince only Sinatraa that forgetting about high school—or college for the time being—and moving across the country into the Selfless house in Atlanta was a good idea; he also needed to convince Sinatraa's mom.

"Hey, we're not creepy," Brad remembered saying to Sinatraa's mom in that first stumbling call. "We're not going to hurt your son." She wanted to know whether this was a viable career path. Brad was very confident that for someone with her son's talents, it was. "Esports is doing well," he had said. *"Counter-Strike* and *League of Legends* are doing well. Salaries are going up, six figures in those games."* The game of *Overwatch* was taking the nation by storm, having already sold 30 million copies in just its first year, but there wasn't yet a league with significant prizes, as OWL had not yet been announced. Brad was relying on his intuition, knowing that the serious professionalization of *Overwatch* play couldn't be far off. He explained to Sinatraa's mother how the success of an esport is heavily correlated with the success of the game: enough copies of *Overwatch* had been sold to make it a competitive esport.

It worked, and Sinatraa and his mother flew to the team's house, a five-bedroom he'd rented because of the large rectangular basement room that would be perfect for computers for practicing.

"We had to clean up the house," Brad admitted reluctantly.

Sinatraa's mother had dinner with the whole team. Brad wanted to show her that he wasn't coaching a bunch of Neanderthals. Dhak, a onetime Miami line cook, made dinner, and they talked long into the evening.

Though Sinatraa and all the early players on the team, who had been practicing together for only a few months, didn't instantly mesh, it took just a few weeks before they began dominating. The turning point had happened in a game against a team called Denial Esports, which featured xQc, one of the most popular *Overwatch* streamers, and Danteh, who would go on to be on the same OWL team as Sinatraa and Dhak. Brad's team was, in Sinatraa's words, "getting shit on again" (i.e., getting dominated), when he said they "all started losing our mind. We couldn't take it anymore." Sinatraa laughed. Of the turning point, he said, "We each got off our heroes and started playing random heroes. Dafran played Soldier for some reason, I stuck with Tracer, and we just ran to their spawn and then started spawn camping them." "Spawn camping" is an attack on the area where opposing players "respawn," or enter the map again after they've died. Five of the Selfless players would wait outside that safe zone and kill anyone who tried to come out while their sixth teammate completed the map objective by himself. The solo player just had to stand somewhere for a while without dying, which was pretty easy because he'd never see an enemy. Pretty much anyone could be the sixth man on this team. After they dominated the rest of the match, a hush descended over the basement room. They realized their crazy strategy actually might work. Then, as Sinatraa said, "We just started wrecking everyone."

The astounding aspect of their strategy was that the five Selfless players spawn camping could overpower six players on the other team. One way to think about this is that Sinatraa, Dhak, and Dafran were each worth 1 ⅕ of an enemy player. Another way to think about it is that Brad's superior scouting ability is worth an extra man. Either way, once they developed the Selfless Comp, they dominated everyone in America, except one: Rogue.

They faced Rogue four times in two months, what Brad described as "an epic run in our rivalry," in four consecutive finals. Each time it was super-close, and each time the ultimate result was the same, 3–2, they lost. Rogue had played in South Korea, and they'd learned something there that Selfless didn't know—they'd learned how to play dive.

According to Brad, Rogue was the only American team that played dive at that time. As a result, they were often immune to the spawn strategy employed by Selfless, because as Brad explained, "You can't spawn-camp dive, because the dive heroes are highly mobile. You can only spawn-camp fat." (Fat means lots of tanks in the composition.) The mobility of the dive heroes created two issues for Sinatraa and Dafran. One was that the Rogue players on D.Va and Winston could simply gang up on one or the other of them—as tank heroes, they both had a lot of health and were hard to kill. These two also closed the distance quickly because of their special abilities. D.Va is a huge pink mech suit with rocket boosters piloted by a nineteen-year-old former esports pro. She protects South Korea from hostile robots. Winston is a superintelligent gorilla scientist who can jump a long distance. He has a lab on the moon. Teams that didn't run these two heroes couldn't get to Dafran or Sinatraa fast enough to kill them before dying, but Rogue often could.

Selfless Gaming tried to run dive, too, after they started experiencing its effectiveness firsthand, but they were not particularly good at it. As Sinatraa explained, "There's a lot that goes into it. Several people have to flank rather than dive, for instance, and the tanks can't take damage before you dive, or they'll just die as soon as they land." I got the sense that in a diplomatic way Sinatraa, known for never throwing anyone under the bus, was acknowledging that their tanks weren't good enough to succeed at the strategy. That would have made sense given how rare top Tracer players were at that time. The most difficult to play, requiring extremely high innate reflexes and processing speed, she was the most in demand and often the top earner on a team. It was easy to see how a coach could prioritize damage players at the expense of tanks.

Messy though his new roommates were, Sinatraa had good influences in the house. Dhak in particular watched out for him, making sure he was eating healthfully (and even cooking for the roommates) and that he worked out regularly.

Dafran was another kind of influence, not negative, more quirky. His only banking account seemed to be PayPal, and the only restaurant nearby that took PayPal was Mellow Mushroom, a pizza place. So what Dafran ate every day for the six months he lived in the Selfless house was chicken pizza. He would order the pizza at 10:00 a.m., smoke a cigarette, down a Coke, retrieve the pizza from the delivery guy, eat one slice, then play *Overwatch*. If he found a player on the enemy team who was streaming their point of view for fans, like Seagull, he would focus on them and destroy them. He would kill the streamer, wait for him to respawn, kill him again, and occasionally tea bag him. Everyone on the stream would see this total unknown, Dafran, shitting on the game's most popular streamer, Seagull. That, in fact, was how Brad had first found him—not by looking at Ladder stats but by watching a popular streamer have each of their attempts to progress in the game systematically dismantled by Dafran. Only then had Brad investigated Dafran and discovered his otherworldly stats and tracking ability.

After Dafran would finish off the streamer of the day, he would close *Overwatch*, go to the player's stream, and watch the whole recording of the match. It was his method of practice, like a hitter watching video of his swing. He could see what he looked like on screen to his prey, so he could adjust his techniques next time. He would watch the video again, then load *Overwatch* again. Play another game. Play, play, play. Kill a streamer. Close the game. Watch the video. And every two hours he would eat a slice of pizza. After sixteen hours, at 2:00 a.m., he would go to bed.

In *Outliers*, Malcolm Gladwell famously popularized the notion, based on a study by psychologist K. Anders Ericsson, that it takes 10,000 hours of deliberate practice to become truly world-class at anything. In the examples he uses to illustrate the principle, he describes a lifetime of work—the Beatles' years of late nights practicing in high school, recording studios, and on tour, Bill Gates honing his coding chops beginning at the age of thirteen. In the 596 days from the release of *Overwatch* to the first

OWL match, based on the 16 hours a day his teammates observed Dafran play when they lived with him, he practiced for 9,536 hours.

Dafran was a touchy subject for everyone involved. His story involves existential dilemmas that strike a nerve in the world of esports, in Dafran's case questions of how the pressure of high-level competitive gaming sixteen hours a day affects the well-being of players and, for league commissioner Nate Nanzer, of the integrity of *Overwatch* competitive play. Brad said that coaching Dafran was difficult. Brad often described himself as "team dad," a role played only sometimes by coaches, other times by managers or an especially "old" player, meaning older than twenty-four. In Dafran's case, Brad had to make real parenting decisions. When Dafran joined the Selfless Gaming house in Atlanta, he was 7,000 miles from his home in Denmark. Some days Dafran wanted to cancel practice, and Brad was obliged to do so. In addition to the $1,500 from Brad, the players streamed for money, and Brad knew that top players with compelling personalities made far more money streaming themselves playing than through tournament winnings or league salaries and that Dafran could use the streaming money. But Dafran's stream was becoming a problem.

That's because, unlike the 90 percent of people who play *Overwatch*, who do so casually in the mode called "Quick Play," Dafran and other elite players played in "Competitive

Play," where players were obsessed with winning and thus ascending the Ladder. Dafran, despite usually being the best player on his team, wasn't always a good teammate. For example, if he perceived his teammates to be "trash," the universal term applied to anyone worse than you, then he would stop trying. He would jump off cliffs to his death or camp out in obscure locations far from the action. Because he was streaming and because he was one of the top-ranked players in the world, his behavior soon came to Blizzard's attention. The issue for Nate Nanzer was that while Dafran was pulling these stunts, Nate was still trying to sell *Overwatch* teams for $20 million, and he was already behind schedule.

The original plan was to launch the league in the fall of 2017. On July 12, 2017, Blizzard announced the first owners who'd forked over $20 million for an OWL franchise. There were only seven of them, not enough to launch the league—they had announced them hoping, no doubt, to attract more buyers. The first seven owners: Robert Kraft, owner of the New England Patriots; Jeff Wilpon, COO of the New York Mets; Andy Miller, co-owner of the Sacramento Kings and NRG Esports; NetEase, Blizzard's Chinese distributor; Kevin Chou, CEO and cofounder of Kabam, a mobile games company; and two esports organizations: Misfits, backed by the founders of the SyFy Channel and the Miami Heat; and Immortals, backed by the film studio Lionsgate, the legendary bond trader Michael Milken, who was sentenced to ten years in prison and fined $600 million in 1989, and a German appliance company. Looking at the investor group, it was clear that both Nate and the teams buying into the league were turning over every rock to find people crazy enough to invest in one of these franchises. And with only seven teams sold and an even number necessary—though the rumor was ten would be it—to start the first season, it was already being pushed back from the fall of 2017 to January 2018.

So when tossed on top of it all, one of the best players in the world was publicly destroying the integrity of Competitive Play on the Ladder, and Nate had to do something serious to show that he wasn't driving a clown car. The final straw came when Dafran, after determining his teammates to be trash, overlaid his Twitch stream with anime porn until the match ended, and his team lost.

Dafran was suspended for a week. During his suspension, Dafran posted on Twitter that he planned to continue his campaign of throwing matches and called for his tens of thousands of followers to do the same. In response, Nate permanently banned Dafran from playing *Overwatch*. Dafran attempted to continue streaming by using different accounts and disguising his IP address. Some poor intern at Blizzard, it seems, was tasked with monitoring Twitch streams, determining which account Dafran was now using, and then suspending that one along with the associated IP address. Eventually Dafran gave up and moved back to Denmark.

On July 28, 2017, Dafran posted his retirement message on TwitLonger, which included the following: "Honestly I am probably going back to Mcdonalds, I would much rather jump from job to job than be a professional player, it is simply not something I enjoy and want to do in the future.... I tried reforming but it simply aint me. I choose to stay true to myself and enjoy what I enjoy, staying a Manchild. We are all different and we all have our things in life that makes it fun to live, money and fame is not everything."

True to his word, Dafran went back to working at McDonald's in Denmark, his job before streaming. Behind the scenes, Brad and Brett also went to work. Brad worked with Dafran's family to persuade him to find a healthier balance to his gaming schedule, which he did. Brett, being close to Nate Nanzer, explained the situation in private and the steps being taken to help Dafran. In October 2017, Nate quietly unbanned Dafran from *Overwatch*, allowing him to earn money from streaming.

By that time, Brad had dissolved Selfless. He had been floating a lot of bills. Rent for the house was $3,500 per month, plus pay for six players at $1,500 per month. When he added utilities and a few meals a day, it totaled close to $15,000 per month, $180,000 per year. That's serious money, and in the end he couldn't pay for it all with what he earned from the team. While the most successful *Overwatch* organizations generally generated revenues in large part based on sponsorship deals (franchising and broadcast hadn't started yet), Selfless tried a different approach, generating all of its revenue instead by selling the player contracts of people Brad had scouted. In the sixteen months that he operated, he sold thirteen player contracts. His team was like a development league for the top organizations, and though he earned $100,000 between two of his best deals, Selfless was a losing investment.

Brad didn't dwell on that, however. Instead, he said he was pleased that he and his assistant coaches were so good at scouting talent that they were able to generate significant revenue so that the financial hit hadn't been worse. It was an experiment, and in Brad's view, he had done everything right. When the team dissolved, in fact, he could have tried to sell Dhak and Sinatraa, likely for enough to turn a profit, but Brad decided to release them instead. Sinatraa was underage, as OWL had announced that players must be eighteen to play. Sinatraa was representing Team USA at the World Cup, where Brad knew he would get a lot of interest from OWL teams already in the league. "I was worried that his age would hurt his interest," Brad said, so he released him. Brad figured that,

CHAPTER 6

DAVID, GOLIATH, AND SINATRAA

In 2013, the first year of Cloud9's existence, Jack Etienne could devote only nights and weekends to his fledgling esports organization. By day, he ran sales at Crunchyroll, a video-streaming platform focused nearly entirely on anime.

The catalyst that sent Jack out of the corporate world and into esports full-time was an acquisition. A company acquired Crunchyroll and wanted to know why the head sales guy, Jack, was getting a 7 percent commission on direct and indirect sales (typically sales commissions are 10 percent on direct sales, and maybe 1 percent on indirect sales, if any). Because nearly all of the company's revenues were from advertising, that is, indirect sales, Jack's deal meant that he alone took home 7 percent of company revenues. Jack had been able to negotiate his unorthodox blended rate because he'd started at Crunchyroll as their first salesman. Because he had built the entire client base, the CEO remained happy with him and honored the deal. But now that the machine was humming, the new owners didn't see the value in paying Jack $1 million a year.

Years later, that CEO would lament to Jack that Jack had received a raw deal in the acquisition, stripped of his income stream just as his four years of hard work were paying off. Jack responded, "Thank God that happened. That's the best thing that ever happened to me." For if he had stayed at Crunchyroll too long, Jack might have missed his opportunity in esports, an opportunity that would come to define his life.

He had left Crunchyroll with a solid cushion of savings but also a newborn daughter. He was very unsure of himself. For fifteen years he'd worked in sales, his only job since graduating college, and now he had to figure out how to make money in esports. He owned only one team at that time, in the North American division of the League of Legends Championship Series (NA LCS), the most popular esports league in the world.

That team provided Jack some reassurance, as they'd won the North American summer split in 2013, taking home

$50,000 and earning a trip to the World Championship, where they placed fifth, pocketing another $75,000. (The NA LCS played two seasons per year: spring and summer. The team that won the summer split playoff earned a spot in the World Championship, as did the team with the best results across both splits.) "That first year was incredible, but it could have been a fluke," Jack said, describing the anxiety he felt as he poured himself into managing Cloud9 full-time. His anxiety would be short-lived. In 2014, Jack's Cloud9 team placed first in the NA spring split, second in the NA summer split, and again placed fifth at the World Championship. Total haul: $150,000 in tournament winnings. Far more important than the prize winnings, though, was the fact that Jack now owned a globally recognized contender, meaning he could sell merchandise and court sponsors.

As Jack was leaving Crunchyroll, Brett Lautenbach, the man who would become president of NRG Sports and therefore Brad's boss, faced his own career dilemma. His final semester in college, he'd been producing commercials and music videos, when a certain incident became his personal nightmare for two weeks: a local band wanting to do a Detroit early dance-house video that required an elaborate wall of tube TVs, which took a toll on his back and an even greater one on his ambition to pursue film production. Once he graduated, he took a job as an assistant to a well-known film festival producer because it sounded acquisition, 2014, Twitch averaged 350,000 concurrent viewers. In 2018, when OWL launched, Twitch averaged more than a million concurrent viewers, an average annual increase of 35 percent. Brett could see the gold rush and that WME was missing out.

It wasn't just eyeballs where there were opportunities but ticket sales as well. The 2013 World Championship for *League of Legends* at the Staples Center, the 15,000-person arena that's home to the Los Angeles Lakers, sold out tickets in less than an hour. Many esports veterans cited this exact moment as the moment they knew that esports was going to take off in the United States.

Jack Etienne's Cloud9 team placed fifth at that tournament, and after attending, he headed back to San Francisco to his day job, Crunchyroll. The winner, SK Telecom, the same organization that took home the €10,000 prize at Dhak's first tournament, the team that employed Lee Sang-hyeok, better known as Faker, the best LoL player ever, took home $1 million.

To convince WME of the opportunity in esports, Brett pitched every angle he could think of—player representation, team representation, running tournaments. They were on a buying spree, having just acquired IMG Worldwide for $2.2 billion in 2013.

He found an organization called Global eSports Management that was doing exactly the kind of business that he believed WME could profit from, reached out to them, and within sixty days they were owned by WME.

The head of Global eSports Management, Tobias Sherman, basically demanded that Brett work for him as a condition of the deal, and they put together an ambitious plan to launch a broadcast TV–based competitive esports league.

The league they created would be available not just to potential network partners, as was typically the case, but also on Twitch, where anyone with an internet connection could stream it for free. When the dual-broadcast idea was brought up, at most networks the notion of giving away free viewership to a competitor digital platform was not well received. At least until they met with Turner. "Tobias had this whole two-page script about how it had to be dual broadcast," Brett recalled. "He got maybe five sentences into his pitch before Turner said, 'Yeah, of course it has to be dual broadcast.'"

That was the origin of ELEAGUE. The league began with *Counter-Strike*, for good reason. On the surface level it's easy to understand—point, shoot, kill—but there was also depth and complexity to the strategy. As you learn more about the game, you start to appreciate when to use your flashbang grenades, how to approach the corners, and so on, in the same way that someone might understand an NFL offense. And even if you might not know why they're running the ball versus throwing the ball, or how they decide when to use a flashbang, you can still follow what's happening.

T-Mobile was the client that helped them launch their esports dreams. Tobias had heard the wireless company was looking for a new agency of record just for esports, so he coordinated a meeting between them and WME's esports and brand strategy groups, where Brett would represent the esports interest. As with every brand he'd talked with before, Brett was sure T-Mobile execs would ask how they could get their intellectual property into the games (e.g., a T-Mobile store inside an *Overwatch* or *Counter-Strike* map), and he was afraid that nongamers at WME might make foolish promises about what they could deliver. The answer to how they could get their intellectual property into these games was simple: they couldn't. Blizzard were as protective of their intellectual property as Disney—there was no chance they would allow brands and logos into their games. Brett was at the meeting in large part to make sure none of his bosses made impossible promises.

WME ended up winning the business. As Brett and his team started their work on the esports strategy for T-Mobile, the rumblings began that Activision-Blizzard were up to something with their new game, *Overwatch*. Brett wondered what the league would look like, thinking it might be a good fit for a T-Mobile sponsorship. T-Mobile wanted a game that was inclusive, and the brightness and futurism of the *Overwatch* aesthetic fit T-Mobile in a way that most popular esports games didn't. By contrast, games like *Counter-Strike* were more realistic, with bloody gore and one team playing as terrorists. Half of CS: GO matches end in the proclamation "Terrorists win." That didn't seem to fit as well. So WME advised T-Mobile that *Overwatch* was probably the game they wanted to get behind, assuming the rumors about Blizzard's ambitious plan for the league were true.

Brett set up the T-Mobile executives with Nate Nanzer to give them more familiarity with the as-yet-unannounced league. Just as this was coming together, Andy Miller, co-owner and operator of NRG Esports, called Tobias, letting him know he was looking for someone to come in to run operations at NRG and wondering whom Tobias might know. "Easy," Tobias said. "You should talk to Brett Lautenbach. He's been a rock star for us, and he told me, literally a week ago, that he wants to learn the team management side." After doing eight interviews in fourteen days, all while keeping on top of his job at WME, Brett called Andy and told him he needed to shit or get off the pot. "I'm flying out to Los Angeles in two weeks," he said, "and my brother lives in San Francisco. I can visit him, and come by Palo Alto while I'm up there. Why don't we wrap this up? Either I'm the guy or I'm not." This bold move paid off. They met, and Brett got the job. He accepted and gave his two weeks' notice at WME the next day. Brett had spent four and a half years at WME. He'd helped the company acquire Tobias's esports agency, landed a major client to assist their push into esports, and launched an entire new esports league. And now that he'd seen the inner workings of the esports industry from the highest level, he wanted to understand what it would be like on the ground, working for a team on which everyone poured everything they had into climbing to the top of the world.

When Brett took over as president, NRG had just lost their LoL team, leaving them with four teams: Overwatch, Counter-Strike, Smite, and Rocket League, as well as an individual playing *Super Smash Bros.* (later *Smash Ultimate*). Over the next two years, Brett would acquire teams or individual players in six more games: *Fortnite, Clash Royale, Hearthstone, For Honor, Dragon Ball FighterZ*, and *Apex Legends.* He saw opportunity in all those leagues, and so he chased it, but he admitted that if he weren't so passionate about gaming, he wouldn't be able to keep up with it. "I have a couple friends at Goldman that tell me they're interested in getting into esports," he said, "because they like playing video games. I tell them, unless you're willing to give your heart and soul, plus your life and your sleep to this, don't do it. It's banking hours, but there's way less money in it."

The day after Brett verbally agreed to give his heart, soul, life, and sleep to Andy, he headed to Blizzard's headquarters in Irvine, California, for the big meeting he'd arranged among Blizzard, his WME bosses, and potential OWL sponsor T-Mobile. Walking Blizzard's campus, where three gleaming white, two-story buildings surround a central courtyard in the center of which is a huge statue of an orc riding a wolf, would have been like walking back in time through the history of esports. Inside the lobby, Brett passed a nine-foot statue of Grommash Hellscream, one of the heroes from *Warcraft II* and *III*. Grommash and other *Warcraft* heroes were so compelling to gamers that they created an entire new game using Blizzard's world-editing tools to strip out the core gameplay elements of resource management and unit production in favor of five-on-five brawls between the game's heroes. These "modded" (from modified) versions of *Warcraft III* were the inspiration for multiplayer online battle arena (MOBA) games, such as *League of Legends* and *Dota*, which would dominate esports for the next decade. Though Blizzard's intellectual property had enabled and inspired these wildly popular and profitable MOBA games, Blizzard hadn't collected a dime.

In MOBA games like *LoL* and *Dota*, the player controls a hero with a unique name, outfit, and abilities, usually a new made-up species. Each hero can be selected by only one player, so a five-on-five match will have ten unique heroes.

The different abilities of the heroes, like the demands of positions on a sports team, were the missing piece that made MOBA games compelling to watch. With so many abilities at their disposal, the composition of each team and the ways in which they work together were just as important as the skill of the players, and so the heroes' differing abilities lay the groundwork for more sophisticated strategy. Instead of being a game close to pure reflex like an FPS, there are now lineup questions and important tactical decisions for the team to make (and coordinate) within each game. This opens the game up to armchair fans, who can question the team's choices in player signings, team dynamics, and strategies. Older esports titles were typically one-player, reflex-driven affairs, where the opportunities for fans to weigh in were more limited: "He should have clicked faster!"

After listening to the pitch that Nate made to T-Mobile, Brett could see that OWL was going to be huge. He was ahead of the curve relative to most of the world, though he was still way behind Jack Etienne, who had by then already been running an Overwatch team for six months. Jack had known he wanted to be in OWL "before it was announced." Like Brett, Jack appreciated how the inviting fantasy aesthetic of the game (i.e., the violence looks cartoony) would allow sponsors to really get behind it, and he had noted that the pro players on Cloud9's various teams in other games were all playing it in their time off.

When teams started forming, Jack was running one of the first large traditional esports companies to get into the game. Jack signed a team called Google Me in March 2016, two months before the game was even released and eight months before he would hear Bobby Kotick's pitch about OWL along with the billionaires at BlizzCon 2016. While Brett had been scrapping at WME, Jack had been scouting and signing players based on their performance in the *closed beta* of *Overwatch*.

It didn't take long for Jack to regret his signing, though. The team he'd almost signed, which he described as "six dudes playing *Overwatch*," had been picked up by rival organization EnVyUs and had won the first OGN *Overwatch* tournament. By far the best esports production network on the planet, OGN was the Korean equivalent of ESPN. OGN had launched what they called the Apex Series for *Overwatch*, which featured the highest level of pro play the game would see until the advent of OWL. The Apex Series would run for only four seasons before Blizzard informed OGN that they'd chosen a different broadcaster for the Overwatch League, shutting it down. Many future OWL stars and even entire OWL teams cut their teeth in the Apex Series (for instance, EnVyUs eventually became the Dallas Fuel in OWL).

Brett, upon reporting for duty at NRG in October 2016, had been immediately shipped to Shanghai for a month, where NRG's Overwatch team was competing in a tournament called APAC. The team had an interesting origin story. It all started when Shaq was at the Consumer Electronics Show as TNT was broadcasting live from the convention. At the same time there was a *Counter-Strike* tournament. Thorin, a legendary CS broadcaster known for his strong personality, got into a little verbal sparring with Shaq. It was a lighthearted dueling-broadcast-desk scenario, the desks maybe about fifty feet apart, with Shaq on the *Inside the NBA* desk with Charles Barkley, Kenny Smith, and Ernie Johnson, while Thorin was on the ELEAGUE desk analyzing the *Counter-Strike* tournament.

Thorin narrated to the camera something about the *Counter-Strike* player ShahZam having popped off during a match, adding within earshot of Shaq, "I'm not talking about *Kazaam*, that terrible movie that Shaq made in the '90s."

There were nervous glances at the TNT desk.

"How quickly can you run?" asked Ernie Johnson. "Because Shaq can cover some ground."

"So you guys think [*Counter-Strike*] is a sport?" Shaq asked, gesturing to Thorin at the esports desk. "I'll challenge you to any game you want. I'll make you eat those words."

"How about weight loss?" responded Thorin. "Should we do that? Is that a sport?"

"What about muscles?" Shaq was laughing now. "What about boxing, if I come over there and punch you? This is America—the queen can't help you over here, buddy." After definitely winning his sparring match with Thorin, Shaq watched some of the *Counter-Strike* tournament. When he got back home, he called his friend Mark Mastrov, the 24 Hour Fitness founder who had cofounded NRG with Andy.

"I just watched *Counter-Strike* and this esports thing," said Shaq. "I watched this team called NRG. It was super fun."

"Yeah, I know it's fun!" said Mark. "That's my team."

"What do you mean?"

"Andy and I started that team, NRG."

"Without me?"

This made Mark laugh. "If you want to do it, you're in."

Shaq was in. On their first investor call, Shaq asked, "Okay, so what's the plan?" to which Andy responded that they needed to find an Overwatch team. "Who's your first choice?" Shaq wanted to know. Andy said they liked a team led by Seagull, because he's the most popular Overwatch streamer in the world. "Okay, done," said Shaq, and sent out a tweet: "Hey @A_Seagull and your @playoverwatch boys. Time to step it up to the @NRG.gg family. We would love to have you all on board. Come on ova." As you can imagine, that got Seagull's attention. He sent his phone number to Shaq, who called him, and kazaam! Like a terrible '90s movie, it was quickly done. Seagull and his boys were now on NRG Esports.

The team finished the APAC tournament in Shanghai in the middle of the pack. Two of the players had had a falling-out, and it seemed like moving forward from there would be all uphill. It was Andy's first experience dealing with players who disliked each other and desperately didn't want to work together, and he learned about how those with different styles could mesh—or not. From there, the team went to Korea for OGN and got knocked out almost immediately. NRG dissolved the team and went back to the drawing board. Shaq giveth, and Shaq taketh away.

Shaq also attracteth, however, and soon many more famous people would invest in NRG. "I think some people might think we have guys who we gave shares to or paid or something," Andy said. "None of that happened. We had Jimmy Rollins right away, Ryan Howard right away. Alex Rodriguez called Mark, because they're friendly as well. Mark knows everybody. Alex asked to put in a lot of money, which he did. He asked for a board seat, so he's on the board." He subsequently brought his future wife, Jennifer Lopez, on board.

From the ashes of the first team's failures, NRG assembled a new team, a much more popular team, pursuing streamers with fan bases and big personalities. They kept Seagull, who fit that profile, and the team started doing really well at scrimmages. But between streaming, tournaments, and practice, Seagull began to burn out. Based on the previous year's performance, NRG had an invitation to OGN Season 2, which was hotly contested. This new iteration of the NRG team hadn't competed in any official tournaments, so fans and rival esports organizations were asking whether NRG really deserved to go to OGN. Seagull decided he wanted to take a break from competitive play until Overwatch League and go back to streaming, which made a lot of sense. If you're burned to a core right before Overwatch League starts, you have little chance of surviving the relentless schedule of a full season. NRG released Seagull and declined to attend OGN's Apex Series Season 2 tournament. Would you believe it, the team that got their spot was Jack Etienne's Cloud9, who would be immortalized in the Overwatch League for their performance there, and not in a good way. One common objective in *Overwatch* matches, called Control, requires a team hold a point for a set amount of time—players must defend the position nervously as a clock ticks up to 100 percent, the clock starts ticking for the opposing team if they recapture it. On three different occasions, Cloud9's opponent, Afreeca Freecs Blue, had ticked their percentage up into the 90s, only for Cloud9 to win a team fight but lose, because none of their players moved onto the requisite point, and the clock just kept ticking to 100. This particular kind of embarrassment would become known as a C9—a failure to secure the objective because you're focused on fighting.

It was at this chaotic period in NRG's *Overwatch* history that Blizzard began sending out signals of an official league on the horizon. Bobby Kotick had begun dropping the bomb on potential owners that teams would cost $20 million. "By the time we got our meeting," Brett says, "it was agonizing. We'd heard other teams had their meeting, and we hadn't been invited to have a meeting yet. Andy and I were pestering Nate to obscene levels."

Finally, Andy and Brett got the nod to come in and have the bomb dropped on them. After the meeting in the Activision-Blizzard boardroom, and now knowing the price, Andy had a lot of questions. How was OWL going to slow the game down to allow people who don't play the game, or more casual fans, to fall in love with *Overwatch*? What was the plan behind the local market? What were the league's revenue projections? Most importantly, why did a team cost so goddamn much?

After deliberating in a coffee shop across the street from Activision's offices about whether this $20 million bet was worth everything they'd invested in NRG and more, Brett and Andy decided they were on board. They could imagine how local markets were going to change the esports game. Suddenly, they would have tickets, apparel, broadcasting revenue, and sponsorships to draw revenue from, in addition to the usual tournament prizes.

Jack Etienne, however nervous he may have been about the large cost, was similarly sold. He first sought commitments from his investors, raising $25 million and securing high-profile investors including World Wrestling Entertainment, the San Francisco Giants outfielder Hunter Pence, the co-owner of the Washington Capitals and Wizards, the cofounder of the talent agency Creative Artists Agency, and the Beverly Hills Sports Council, a baseball agency.

He negotiated with Blizzard and became the owner of the London team. It would be the only OWL team in the UK, and Jack felt good about the attention that could bring. "I basically have an entire country," Jack said. "They've got great infrastructure for transit, so we could have games in London, games in Manchester. There's all sorts of places we could go and massive crowds could come, too, relatively easily." All that motivated him to have a world-class team. Recognizing that he didn't have that, Jack started over. He was unsure where to get players, wanting to try to build a team in Korea but also wanting to keep an open mind. He had open tryouts in Korea as well as coaches scouting for talent in North America and Europe. Ultimately, Jack and Brett would arrive at the same conclusion about the first player they should sign: Sinatraa.

In the summer of 2017, when Sinatraa was playing for Selfless, he had been chosen to represent the United States in the Overwatch World Cup. "It was a tryout, and I think they picked thirty players," Sinatraa said of making the team. He did well in the tryout. "I never got subbed out, I played Tracer and a little bit of Zarya." The US World Cup coach, Kyle Souder, better known as KyKy, had played for Jack's Cloud9 team for nine months in 2016, later becoming the coach of EnVyUs. Because of that team's success, KyKy got the nod for the World Cup coaching gig. In addition to Sinatraa, KyKy chose a player named Adam he'd played with on Jack's Cloud9 team, two players named Rawkus and FCTFCTN from FaZe Clan (a team that eleven-year-old Sinatraa once tried to get signed to on the basis of 720 no-scope headshots), Jake Lyon, gamertag JAKE, and Matt Iorio, better known as Coolmatt. Being chosen for the US World Cup team in 2017 was fortuitous. Four of the players would be signed by the Houston OWL franchise: JAKE, Rawkus, Coolmatt, and FCTFCTN. The fifth starter, Adam, was already signed to Cloud9. That left Sinatraa.

"The World Cup was in a hangar with a big crowd for group stage," Sinatraa told me. The hangar in question, the Barker Hangar at the Santa Monica Airport, was also used in the Championship Gaming Series debacle. It's 35,000 square feet, vaulting forty-three feet at the center.

From August 11 to 13, the US team dominated their group stage, beating New Zealand 4–0, Brazil 4–0, Taiwan 3–1, and Germany 3–0.

In the meantime, Brett had discovered Brad, but he didn't yet hire him to be coach. Brett once explained his approach to building a team by saying, "We knew we had some months before we thought Bobby and Nate were going to start talking to teams formally, and we thought, 'Let's go learn everything we can, and make every mistake humanly possible in *Overwatch*. So we can learn all of our lessons before we get into Overwatch League.'" Presumably, that is how they made their first two mistakes: the Shaq team and the popular streamer team.

In addition to trying out multiple team-building strategies, NRG would cycle through multiple *Overwatch* coaches, first hiring Seamoose in May 2017. "Seamoose was a good coach early on," Brett said. "He came off recommendations of some of our players. It was working well, and then during this time of bringing in new players, it felt like (1) it was dragging, and (2) it wasn't the most thought out. We were one of the first teams out there looking at talent. We felt like if we had that advantage, we needed to execute on it. It felt like we were letting it slip through our fingers. We started to think maybe he's not the guy." In July 2017, Brett started looking around for new coaching options and began the conversation with

Brad. Brad's Selfless Gaming had caught his eye with a major run of championships at the lower tiers of Overwatch in the United States, winning with players he paid $1,500 per month, while Cloud9, EnVyUs, and NRG were paying $4,000 per month.

At first, Brett brought Brad to the team to supplement Seamoose on a two-week trial. Those two weeks went exceedingly well. "I really appreciated Brad's sentiment about how he looked at pro players in the game, and his scouting," Brett said. "That's always a hard thing in esports. We don't have farm leagues traditionally, and things like that. You get in this habit of recruiting from the known quantities and not recruiting from the unknown quantities. Brad was like, 'look, there's known quantities, there's semi-known quantities, and there's total unknowns. Total unknowns you see on the leaderboards but nobody really talks to.' Brad was like, 'I don't want to just go with known quantities. I want to be able to recruit and look at guys that other people might have doubts about, that other people might not think are up to the task, maybe they're hard to work with, etc.'" Brett bought into that recruiting method, and along with Andy, he decided Brad was a better option as head coach. They hired him. Next, they had to build a winning team from the ground up.

Deciding to name the team San Francisco Shock, Brett and Brad quickly turned to the recruitment stage, seeking to fill every position on the new team. The only player from the popular streaming team who would remain on the roster was Iddqd, whom management had wanted to keep in order to provide a sense of continuity, even though Brad wasn't sure he was good enough to start on the team. The first player Brad went after was Dhak, the world-class Lucio, who was essential to a competitive *Overwatch* team. Next Brad wanted Sinatraa. Sinatraa was more than just a damage god. "If you ever watch Sinatraa try hard in a scrim or practice," Brad said, "sometimes he just takes over leading the team. He'll start shot-calling, he'll start calling comp changes, he has this ability in him, when he wants to turn it up, to go from being this quiet little kid to being this commanding presence on the team." Still, he was a long-term prospect. With OWL's eighteen-and-over requirement, Sinatraa would miss the first eighteen matches of the forty-match season. Still, Sinatraa was someone that Brad believed he could build a franchise around for years, not needing to worry about the reflexes of his Tracer until at least 2024. As Sinatraa grew up, if he became that commanding presence on top of his innate talent and work ethic, Brad reasoned his team would never be out of contention. It didn't hurt that Sinatraa had a popular stream and would bring a fair number of fans with him.

At the same time that Brad had again set his sights on Sinatraa, this time for an OWL spot, so had Jack Etienne.

The bidding war that resulted is a hypersensitive subject for all parties involved. Brett would say of it only that it was the worst week of his professional life. He said that he and Jack had since "buried the hatchet." But who was wielding the hatchet? The first time I asked Jack about the Sinatraa bidding war, he froze in place and provided no comment. Later, when we sat for a formal interview, he still wouldn't divulge the details.

On September 3, 2017, Jacob Wolf of ESPN posted the headline "NRG Signs 17-Year-Old Overwatch Pro Sinatraa for $150K." As Jacob wrote, "The high salary comes after a dispute between NRG Esports and Cloud9, which both attempted to complete agreements with the player, sources said. Through a competitive bidding war that raised the salary by nearly $50,000, Sinatraa and his mother—who is required to sign the agreement because he is a minor—ultimately signed with NRG."

A rumor with unidentifiable origins circulated among the press that Jack offered $175,000, to which Sinatraa's agent told him that he was going to sign with Shock for $150,000. Whatever the ultimate cost, the competition over Sinatraa had been hot for a reason. He was the top US player for a competitive team on a crucial hero, a hero with such a high skill requirement that only a handful of players in the world could pilot her at the top level of play. In the end, Sinatraa's decision to join NRG's Shock would decide the fates not only of individual players vying for the same spot but of three different teams in the Overwatch League. One of those three teams would win the championship.

When I asked Brett why he thought Sinatraa had signed with Shock for less money, he talked about the effectiveness of their pitch. He didn't mention Brad and Dhak. Jack, who had suspicions that NRG used something secret outside of his contract to lure Sinatraa in, didn't mention Brad and Dhak either. When I asked Sinatraa, he also didn't mention the two guys he'd spent the past year with as a reason to join Shock. But, ignoring the fact that Sinatraa had spent his first eight months away from home, at the age of sixteen, with Brad and Dhak strikes me as odd. It's easy to believe that Sinatraa took less money to play for Shock because he wanted to stick with Brad and Dhak. And there's nothing wrong with that.

Losing Sinatraa didn't by any means sink Jack. Though at one point Sinatraa was his greatest heart's desire, he'd actually been only the second among four of Jack's heart's desires. In contrast to NRG, which drew primarily from North America, Cloud9 was global. Jack had coaches recruiting not just in America and Europe but in Korea as well.

"During our tryouts in Korea we identified two players who we definitely wanted," Jack said, referring to NUS and Fury. They were free agents, and they formed the backbone of a decent Korean team that won some scrimmages but couldn't win at the top tier. Somewhere along that process, another Korean team, called KongDoo, which had performed well in the Apex Series but hadn't won a spot in OWL, reached out to Jack and offered to sell him their players. They were easily Top 4 in the world at that time, and many people thought they could be #1. After an extensive negotiation, they finally reached an agreement that worked for everyone, and Jack added KongDoo's best four players to his roster—Birdring, Bdosin, Fissure, and Rascal.

When the new team tried to play together, they got blasted by a Korean team called GC Busan in the early rounds of the final Apex tournament. Jack wanted a piece of the talent that beat him, and he set his sights on buying GC Busan—adding its best players to his team. After checking with his players and making sure they were on board with his plans for a large roster, Jack signed the entire GC Busan team as they were on their way to winning the Apex finals.

Sinatraa's acquisition by Shock had caused Jack to pivot to Korea, signing first KongDoo, then GC Busan. The third team affected by Sinatraa's choice to go to Shock was the Houston Outlaws, which, despite signing four of the six Team USA players, not only failed to sign Sinatraa but failed to sign any Tracer at all. This would come to haunt them.

Houston were, despite their ambitions, the team that it seemed couldn't do anything right. At the end of the first season, one analyst would comment to me, "The Outlaws could've done better, the tragic story line there was their ability to always choke at the end. Always lose that king of the hill map....And their insisting on not needing a Tracer: I think that was what made it almost comical at the end. They were flexing every damage they had onto Tracer, claiming that we don't need a main Tracer. It was as if they had their hearts so set on Sinatraa that after he'd been scooped up they couldn't bear to even look at another Tracer."

Not every would-be esports mogul who got a one-on-one meeting with Bobby and Nate came away excited about OWL. One of those less enthused was Andy Dinh, founder and CEO of Team SoloMid. He'd hired a player named Blam to put together a new OWL team. The team would never materialize, and on May 5, Blam posted on Twit-Longer, "After learning more information about the OWL ($$$), TSM decided that it'd be better for the organization to stay out of the competitive scene, at least for now." TSM's decision to decline to join OWL made news. After all, Andy Dinh was well respected in esports, having started as a pro *League of Legends* player himself, winning third at the first-ever LoL World Championship in 2011.

To some, even legitimate fans of esports, the $20 million number for an OWL team seemed insane, far more than was ever offered for something considered such a gamble. Uber's Series A round of fundraising, for instance, was $11 million; Facebook's Series A round was $13 million; and Google's Series A was $25 million. How on earth was a marginally profitable esports organization supposed to raise that kind of money? And, given the rumors that Blizzard would be keeping the bulk of the league's profits for themselves and claiming first rights to sponsors, would the league *ever* even be profitable enough to justify a $20 million investment?

It helped that the $20 million price tag would be spread over a number of years, meaning the initial payment would be something more like $5 million. But with the player salaries, health care, housing, insurance, utilities, gaming equipment, and so on added on top of that, it was a serious commitment of capital to esports, a hitherto losing bet. Wealthy tycoons including the Lacobs, the owners of the Golden State Warriors, couldn't get comfortable with the investment.

Still, OWL found enough investors to build the league they wanted. For the first season, there would be twelve teams, their preseason rankings largely determined by their performance in OGN's now-terminated Apex Series. Seoul were considered the favorite going into the season, with Spitfire ranked second by ESPN's preseason power rankings and the New York Excelsior (NYXL) ranked third. These Top 3 teams were made up of all Korean players. After them, there wasn't much consensus in the rankings. Anyone could emerge.

CHAPTER 7

BEAUTIFUL DOWNTOWN
BURBANK

In 1972, Johnny Carson put a small city north of Los Angeles on the map by making fun of it on *The Tonight Show:* in his classic deadpan, Carson described the tract homes surrounding the new studio as "beautiful downtown Burbank." For thirty-seven years and 5,000 broadcasts, Burbank would remain the show's home, until one of Carson's successors moved it back to New York in 2009, an event that the mayor of Burbank described as leaving "a portion of our heart...now empty."

Eight years later, that empty place in the heart of Burbank Studios was finally filled by the next big thing to arrive:

esports. The old *Tonight Show* studio was transformed into Blizzard Arena, a 350-person mini-stadium where every match of the first season of OWL would be played before a live audience and broadcast to the rest of the world on Twitch.

The set inside the arena was sparse: two tables onstage, each with six computers, a broadcast table off to the side, and a few cameras made up all the physical objects in the room. The only parts of the players directly visible to the audience were the tops of their heads just over their computer monitors, meaning that all the physical movements of the players—keyboard strikes, mouse clicks, and frantic scrolling—had to be inferred from the action on the enormous screen above their heads. Twenty feet tall and fifty feet wide, the screen curved and extended twenty feet out into the auditorium, surrounding spectators in the floor seats. The sound system was similarly all-consuming, as much felt as heard. The effect of the screen and sound combined crowded out any ability for conversation or even coherent thought. You just had to lean back and let the spectacle blast you.

Leaving the arena after an OWL game, after recovering from the disorienting quiet of the traffic, one might notice that Burbank in fact *has* a downtown. The average age of an esports fan is twenty-four. There had never been a point in their lives when Johnny Carson's joke about the tract homes made sense.

The first match of the Overwatch League featured the

San Francisco Shock versus the Los Angeles Valiant. Valiant were run by a 900-IQ, Marxist college dropout named Noah Whinston, who was somewhat vague about how he came to own an esports organization worth tens of millions of dollars. When pressed, Noah described the series of events that involved him founding Immortals, the group that purchased the LA Valiant OWL franchise, as "an opportunity," one that allowed him to work with a few LA-area investors. His background before Immortals had been in data-driven sports betting, where he used statistics and data analysis to predict the outcomes of baseball games against the spread. When he started Immortals, he used those same skills to build the first iteration of the roster.

By all accounts, it wasn't one of those situations where rich parents gave their sports-betting kid a job running the San Francisco 49ers. Noah had to round up investors, which included the band Linkin Park, the film studio Lionsgate, and Meg Whitman, former CEO of Hewlett Packard, who sat on the board of Immortals. Although that might have proved an impossible task to most Marxists who didn't graduate from college, Noah was the kind of person you could sense was way beyond you in terms of cognitive ability within about thirty seconds of meeting him.

The first-ever Overwatch League match did not start off well for the San Francisco Shock. They lost the first two maps and thus were halfway to being defeated. Teams always played four maps, only playing a fifth map if they were tied 2–2. (The maps are fictional locations inspired by real-world places. For instance, the map Hanamura is an ancient Japanese village filled with cherry blossom trees. One of the most arresting features of the Blizzard Arena was the beginning of a new map, when suddenly the entirety of the huge digital screen became dedicated to the map environment. On Hanamura, pink cherry blossom petals appeared to float down into the crowd.) Each of the maps that a match alternated through had one of four objectives: pushing a cart, capturing territory, assaulting territory being defended, or a hybrid of capturing territory and then pushing a cart. Each team got a crack at both sides of each map. For instance, on a cart map, first one team attempted to push the cart. They made it as far as they could until time ran out, then the teams switched sides. Whoever pushed the cart the farthest won the map. After the first two maps, the commentators on OWL's broadcast singled out Dhak, saying, "If you want to see the San Francisco Shock make a comeback in this second half, we gotta go to the player they signed first on the roster. It's the old man Dhak. He's one of the best Lucios we have seen in the game. Unfortunately, though, he has not had a ton of time on Mercy. There were a few moments that were a little off for him."

Although securing the map determined who won a game of *Overwatch*, the way to get there was by winning incremental battles, keeping your teammates alive, and killing those on the opposite team. If your team continuously killed the other team and never died, then it should be no surprise even to nongamers that your team would win, because no one can accomplish an objective when they're dead. Ideally, you would want to go into combat with your whole team in order to protect each other, which meant that if one of your teammates accidentally wandered into the path of the enemy sniper and received a high-velocity round to the head, the whole team sat around waiting for their dead teammate to respawn before reengaging the enemy team. There were many exceptions to this, though, such as when the clock was running out or when a player flanked the opposing team or sneaked into their back line (e.g., Sinatraa's goal playing Tracer), and in those situations many different strategies came into play. But the most frequent fighting involved six-versus-six team battles, and the single most important factor in winning those battles was the composition of the teams. (Some comps were simply extremely advantaged against other comps based on hero abilities, mobility, health levels, damage output, and combos of hero ultimate abilities.) The second-most-important factor was how well the team worked together. Did the damage players focus their fire on the same enemy? Did the healers get to their near-death teammates in time to save them? Did the tanks coordinate pushes together? The final factor was how well the individuals performed. How many headshots did the damage land instead of body shots? Did the healers stay all of 2016 and 2017 playing Lucio. Mercy had been virtually unplayed on the pro scene until September 2017, when the fans finally prevailed on Jeff Kaplan, head of game design of *Overwatch*, to improve (buff) her. Players who enjoyed Mercy as a character (she's a gorgeous blonde Swiss doctor, who sports angel wings and a halo in her role as field medic) wanted to be able to pick her without being laughed off the team. In buffing this hottie for the fans, Jeff Kaplan went too far: Mercy immediately became a 100 percent pick-rate hero in elite competitive play. Lucio was no longer meta. It was the dawn of the Mercy meta, causing Dhak to reflect on how, as the election of Chávez in Venezuela had forced him to move to Spain, his life continued to be at the mercy of powerful men making decisions in what they perceived to be the common interest.

Based at least in part on Dhak's limited grasp of Mercy, Shock lost to Valiant 0–4. Still, he didn't get an unfair portion of the blame. In a pro match, teamwork was so important that no single player was fully responsible for any loss (unless they were tilted and trying to lose), though sometimes a single player could pull a victory out of a hat by single-handedly winning a team fight at the end of a match. Matches were first to three wins, though the fourth map still had to be played even if a team had already lost 0–3, a situation known as the "map of shame." Blizzard claimed that the point of the fourth map was for a tie-breaking statistic called the map differential (the number of maps won minus the prior year. It was far above anyone's expectations, perhaps Twitch most of all. The broadcast deal Nate struck with Twitch was based on an estimated concurrent viewership of 50,000 per match, and there were very advantageous (for Blizzard) escalators built into the contract. With the escalators, OWL could earn much more than the $45 million, and there were almost ten times as many viewers as expected during the first match. After the wild success of OWL in its first week, there were whispers of various pieces of office furniture being hurled down hallways at Twitch headquarters.

The first time I met Brad and the Shock players, they were preparing to take the team photos mandated by the league, wearing their official team uniforms: thin orange Capilene jerseys on top of tapered black sweatpants. Their jerseys and sweatpants were pressed—who knew that pressed sweatpants could look stylish?—and they looked sharp if perhaps somewhat retro and slightly unusual, like an extremely fit bowling team.

They milled around chatting, waiting for the call to head to makeup in their official Blizzard Arena training room, a long rectangle with twelve computer stations, six along each long wall. I was most impressed by the ceiling air-conditioning system, which looked like something from a Ridley Scott movie as designed by NASA. I'd expected there to be a certain funk to the practice room given the dozen or so dudes in there practicing for ten hours a day, but it seemed that Blizzard had thought of everything.

Later in the makeup room, where players prepared for the photo shoot, I met Sleepy, who played Zenyatta, a crucial support character that was played in 80 percent of league matches. Sleepy's hair was so black it looked dyed, and the sly expression and tired eyes that helped earn him his nickname gave him something of an emo vibe. Relative to the other players, he was slightly stocky, though they were all in good shape. I would later learn that they're considered "hunky" by their fans, and over the course of the season the walls of the training room would be covered with fan art from their admirers, some of it quite good, capturing the look and spirit of the players often in an anime-inspired style.

I asked Sleepy whether what Andy told me about him was true, that he fell asleep during dinner with him. That his gamertag was a literal description of him. "Yeah," he said, yawning. The topic was old hat.

We moved out of makeup to the arena to wait for the team before them, the Houston Outlaws, to finish their pictures. With all the seats empty, it felt much bigger. From the point of entering the arena until the Outlaws filed out, an uncharacteristic hush fell over the Shock players. I caught a couple of meaningful stares between Shock players and their Outlaws counterparts. As soon as they exited, the quiet room immediately began buzzing with good-natured trash talk, directed, as usual, at fellow teammates. At one point, Danteh, the team's Tracer player until Sinatraa turned eighteen, asked the photographer whether he was allowed to move. He'd followed the photographer's direction to hold still much more diligently than his teammates and had been frozen there like a statue for close to ten minutes. As soon as he asked the question, his teammates began to erupt with rejoinders. "Are you flexing your legs, Danteh?" "Danteh, are you even breathing?" "Dude, your legs must be so tired from that flex, bro."

After the photo shoot, the guys asked whether Danteh needed to be carried, because of his legs. He demurred. When we got back to the training room, Super, another minor, who would turn eighteen ten days after Sinatraa, showed me how to play *Runescape* while the other players practiced. "Don't put this in the book," the team manager, Jaime Cohenca, advised. Jaime later would tell me he was not actually the team manager. He was trying to go pro in *Overwatch* and in fact was currently a Top 500 player in North America. He'd been offered the official role of manager but didn't "feel there was a lot of upward mobility" in it. Instead, he accepted a job as an account manager for Shock's corporate sponsors, though the team manager job continued to stalk him, usually in the form of players asking Jaime to drive them around or pick up dinner and Jaime being too much the helpful type to say, "That's not my job."

I got the sense that the Outlaws were the only team in the league that Shock felt a rivalry with going into the season. Though nobody outright said this to me, there was an unmistakable change in tone whenever Outlaws came up in conversation. The origins of this rivalry were unclear, but it could have been the result of the baggage from when the future Shock players were scrapping to get into the league, their futures uncertain, while the Houston Outlaws players were courted by half the league because they played on the 2017 US World Cup Team. World Cup players received media training and had stage time in front of an 8,000-person crowd during the finals at BlizzCon 2017. They were all American, and many team owners liked the idea of a full team of American players, thinking they'd be easier to market. By the end of the season, the mistakes of that strategy would prove obvious.

Houston's star player, JAKE, was an instant hit with the fans, and he was quickly chosen by Nate Nanzer as the face of the Overwatch League. That meant that he, along with his Outlaws teammate Rawkus, got to appear on *The Today Show*. That his growing fame wasn't based entirely on his talents—and may have been in part the result of his Leonardo DiCaprio–esque looks and the fact that he was a good face for the league, a player who despite his success as a professional gamer spoke openly about aspiring to go to college to study philosophy—perhaps got under the skin of the other teams. Sinatraa, also American, was universally considered a better player than JAKE and would have had a claim to be upset, though he seemed more comfortable out of the spotlight.

Sinatraa would have been a perfectly fine face of the league, too. Tall and thin, the product of a Korean father and German mother, he kept his hair neat and had a way of sidling when he walked that emphasized his lankiness. Beyond that, he was very nice, if a bit standoffish. Sure, he might refer to every rival as "trash," but in fairness, he *was* one of the best *Overwatch* players in the world. But despite his star status, Sinatraa remained a figure more celebrated behind the scenes than onstage, some said, because of what they described as toxic behavior. That included yelling at his teammates for playing poorly after a loss, taunting his opponents after killing them by waving at them and saying, "Hiya," spray-painting the word "Sorry" on the ground next to their dead bodies, or "tea bagging" them.

The other star who took the league by storm in its first season would be xQc, Félix Lengyel, a Canadian tank player on the Dallas Fuel and a one-man nightmare for OWL's public relations department. One of the most popular *Over-watch* streamers—20,000 people watched him every time he played—he was an excellent player, though not the best, maybe not even Top 12 in the world at his position of main tank. But xQc excelled at streaming for a different reason, beyond his skillful gameplay—he was uniquely entertaining. In one video, he stopped playing *Overwatch* to pontificate

Nate to be the on-air interviewer and analyst for OWL, making her the only talent employed full-time by Blizzard, as everyone else, including MonteCristo, was a contractor.

Eight days into the inaugural season of the Overwatch League, the Houston Outlaws defeated the Dallas Fuel 4–0, and Soe's post-match interview would set the league's first scandal in motion. She chose to interview Muma, Houston's openly gay main tank. At the end of his interview, Muma, in an adorably awkward and endearing manner, with a bit of a stutter owing to his excitement, summed up the match by saying, "In the wise words of a good friend of mine, rolled and smoked my doggies." It was xQc's catchphrase, and xQc would not appreciate Muma using it against him. The slight was only exacerbated by the fact that xQc hadn't even been given the chance to play in an OWL match. He'd remained on the bench for the loss to Houston.

In response, the following day on his stream, xQc said, "You didn't smoke shit. Shut your fucking mouth, go back there, suck a fat c***, I mean, you would like it, but…"

On the video, he appears to realize he's crossed a line and stops. But despite his belated self-awareness, his comment rang wrong on so many levels. For one, Muma was nineteen years old, two years younger than xQc and already in a courageous but fragile position as openly gay in gaming. The terms "gay" and even "faggot" were still prevalent in the language of gamers, despite the efforts of civilized people, and

Blizzard, to stomp them out. To make matters worse, xQc was the popular, edgy kid, whose words would resonate with many young fans. In fact, when Muma referenced "the wise words of a good friend of mine" in his interview, there seemed to have been some aspiration in those words. Muma may have thought he was engaging in good-natured shit talking with the closest thing OWL had to a celebrity player, someone he probably hoped to be friends with one day. But xQc's mean-spirited, homophobic reaction broke the rules of friendly trash talk. That was not how banter worked in the esports world; if you were going to develop a catchphrase, then you had to fully expect it to be used against you.

Within days, xQc was suspended from the league. The incident would cast a pall over team shit talking for the rest of the inaugural season.

Meanwhile, after losing to Valiant in the first match of league play, Shock beat the Shanghai Dragons, lost to the Philadelphia Fusion, and then beat Boston. Heading into their fifth match against the London Spitfire, they were 2–2, the Spitfire 4–0. The analysts said Shock would have to "climb a mountain" to get the win. Fissure got the start in this match for Spitfire, with Monte noting him as "the best tank of 2017."

Because of OWL's age rules, Danteh continued to take Sina-traa's spot in the lineup, and he proved to be a surprising bright spot in an otherwise mediocre lineup. Although Danteh popped off against Spitfire, it wouldn't be enough. Spitfire's standout Winston player, Fissure, significantly outplayed his counterpart on Shock, achieving seventeen kills and fifteen deaths, versus ten kills and thirty-one deaths for Nomy, who was Shock's Winston until Super turned eighteen. In this second collision between Brett and Jack, Jack won decisively. Despite playing well, it would be the last match that Fissure ever played for Spitfire.

Falling to 2–3, Shock were mostly left out of contention, unable to succeed at the highest level without their star Tracer, Sinatraa, or up-and-coming tank player Super. They won only one of their final five matches, beating the lowly Florida Mayhem, to finish 3–7 in Stage 1.

If Shock and their long-term strategy in signing Sinatraa were a case study on how *not* to win the inaugural season of Overwatch, Spitfire's season progressed like a study on how to do it. When Spitfire finally met preseason favorite Seoul Dynasty—the only other team that seemed a worthy rival—both teams had lost only once. Seoul were 5–1, Spitfire 6–1. Seoul rostered a damage player named Fleta, widely considered the best player in the league at the time. Before the match, Bdosin described the match's "big expectations," saying that Seoul Dynasty's Fleta needed to "watch his head." After the match, the desk called it the match of the week. It was exactly what the highest level of Overwatch was supposed to look like: perfectly coordinated teamwork in dives, followed by a perfectly executed defense. Players combining two ults simultaneously to wipe out half the enemy team, only for them to be resurrected by Valkyrie. Every battle hung by a string, and nearly every victory hinged on a nearly unbelievable individual play that left even the casters astonished—a headshot on an enemy jumping across a small gap directly overhead, D.Va using her special ability to eat enemy ults at point-blank range, perfectly executed Winston jumps to finish off a healer, and blindingly fast Tracer-on-Tracer battles. Despite the feeling that every battle could have gone either way, Spitfire won 4–0. Though Spitfire would pass Seoul in the league rankings, New York Excelsior remained the team to beat.

If you don't believe pro *Overwatch* players when they tell you that they started playing video games at the age of two or three or four, which they will eagerly tell you, then watching an OWL game should convince you. The moves are so sudden and seamless that key turning points might be missed by an untrained eye, the reactions so automatic that you get the sense they could beat most other *Overwatch* players trying to see through a veil. It is hard not to wonder, however, what could have first attracted them to video games as toddlers and then why this game must have been so appealing to them at a young age. Was it the satisfaction of mastering a system, the escape, the easy topic of conversation it provides to turn strangers into friends? These are questions they didn't talk about as it was obvious to them: their love of gaming was innate, and this game was fun.

Back to the photo shoot now completed, Super and Sinatraa, the two not-yet-eighteen-year-olds, had no good reason to stay at Blizzard Arena while the rest of their team scrimmed. So I offered to give them a ride to their apartment. Jaime came with me, likely more to keep an eye on the kids and the writer than because he actually needed a ride. On the way, I got a sense through Super of why the fast movements of gaming became his passion.

Obviously brilliant, Super spoke quickly, almost impatiently, beginning to answer any question I asked him immediately as it ended, with no break, like he had been preparing his answer while I long-windedly and needlessly finished the question. He also spoke in the manner of someone whose mind is running well ahead of the speed a mouth can move, someone who can process information at twice the rate of a normal person.

I asked him when he thought he might be able to play. "Soon," he said. His skills were ready for OWL. "I was playing *Team Fortress*," he added, "and I thought my mechanics were pretty good. Competitive Season 1 I got Top 500 with my old computer, which was great given how shitty the computer was." His old computer had been able to process the game only at a rate of less than thirty frames per second, which made reacting to opponents a challenge.

Super and Jaime proceeded to compare their former rankings and bicker about who had been better back then, while Sinatraa ignored them, looking at his phone.

"Shut your mouth," Super said.

"I'm just saying I was better," Jaime replied.

"Who's better now?" Super said. "And who was always better?" he added in rapid staccato. It was true that Jaime had once been ranked higher than Super in North America, but there were mitigating circumstances: Super's computer. "The minimum hardware you need is 144 frames per second with a 144-hertz monitor," Super explained. "That's the minimum for pro gamers these days. Thirty FPS was fine for playing with my friends, but there would have been no way that I would have been able to compete at the top level." Even with a 30-FPS computer, Super was one of the top few hundred players in North America, so Super and his father had decided to upgrade it, spending about $1,200 on top-of-the-line hardware. "The GPU [graphics processing unit] I got was $450 alone," Super said. "It's more now, because of the demand from Bitcoin miners."

When he got his new computer, he started quickly getting better. "We used to watch *Overwatch* tournaments all the time," he said. Eventually, he and his friends decided to form a team. The first tournament they played, they were matched against Complexity, one of the best teams at the time. Super's team ended up winning the first map but losing the series. Still, winning that first map showed his potential, and he and his friends started practicing every day.

Super did not, it turns out, need to convince anyone that he should be a pro gamer instead of going to college. "I'm one of the very few people in the world with enough talent to do this professionally," he said, and he thought it was a no-brainer to do it.

My only condition for the ride was that I didn't have to navigate. I never knew how tremendously old it would make me feel to voice it. "Okay, I'll connect to your Bluetooth," Sinatraa offered in response. I had to explain to him that the car was from 2002, "pre-Bluetooth." Then it dawned on me that Sinatraa was from 2000. He was two months old when I graduated from high school. I could be his dad. Instead, I was chauffeuring him home, and in general following him around, observing him like an understudy, hoping he would drop his guard to answer just one more of my questions.

No Bluetooth was too much for Sinatraa, so he told Jaime to do the navigating. I got the sense that Jaime had to do a lot of things like this. Sinatraa and Super were the stars, and they expected some soft-glove treatment. Jaime told me later he was slowly morphing into the team manager against his will. Officially, Jaime was the account manager for NRG's sponsors—Logitech, Republic of Gamers (a chip/board product line made by Asus), and Events DC—but neither he nor Sinatraa nor Brad nor I was under the illusion that that was why he got out of bed every morning and hauled himself to the arena. Those sponsors—the dominant maker of gaming keyboards and mice, which makes sense as a sponsor, as well as a convention, sports, and entertainment events company, which doesn't—pointed to one of the obstacles that esports leagues had long had in getting funded: fans are mostly males in their twenties, the type of guys who always used ad blockers and had never subscribed to cable. The only premium or lucrative product they seemed to regularly consume was video games. Or, perhaps for Dafran, pizza.

On the drive, Sinatraa kept us updated on his social-media feed. One of the *Overwatch* streamers he followed had done something ill-advised and had begun reading the comments that viewers wrote on his stream, including one that said, "I hate all the blecks." I didn't understand it at first, assuming "blecks" was gamer slang I haven't learned. Nope: pure racism.

"Wow," I remarked. "That's no good."

Sinatraa shook his head. "Terrible. . . . What an idiot."

Had I said the right thing, and had these gaming protégés with their still-plastic brains properly registered my outrage? Within a few minutes, we had moved on, but I kept wondering. With so few adults around in their lives—and those who were often acting subservient to them—I started to feel an obligation to set some kind of example.

Eventually, Super broke the silence. "I miss Brent," he said, as if we had been privy to the train of thought that had led there.

"The guy that got fired for sexual assault?" I asked, probably unwisely.

"No, that was Max." Max Bateman, the prior manager of Shock, was accused of sexual assault by a Twitch streamer in a TwitLonger post, which read in part, "My last drink was made by Max at the table.... At this point I felt dizzy, confused," followed by details of the alleged assault. Andy had fired him immediately. Max denied the allegations in a TwitLonger post, saying he'd cooperated with investigators. In response, the streamer wrote, "I filed a police report after but I was told there wasn't enough proof/evidence." Max wasn't charged.

Jaime steered us to safer ground, explaining that they had hired Brent to produce content. "He reps social media influencers," he said. "Smart dude, but it didn't work out. He's talented, just couldn't produce good content. Maybe too disorganized."

Super agreed but dissented to add that he liked him and he missed him. I wasn't sure what to make of this from

Super. Was he saying he wanted to rehire Brent? Was it a veiled dig at Jaime, whom he might not like as much?

Although I may have been reading into nothing in thinking there could be tension between Super and Jaime, it was certainly true that among the players themselves on Shock there were very clear preferred pairs. Dhak and Babybay were the workout dudes; Nevix and Nomy, the solid, compassionate tanks; Sleepy and Danteh, the quiet teenagers; and Super and Sinatraa, the guys who couldn't play yet. And then there was Iddqd, the one guy who had made it from Brad's original *Overwatch* team to Shock, only to fall completely off the map. Brad's initial read of Iddqd's skill level proved accurate: Babybay was strictly better at every character that Iddqd played, and so he didn't have a role. They kept Iddqd on the team's roster, where he made money streaming *Overwatch*, but didn't force him to attend practices or even matches at Blizzard Arena, which seemed almost cruel. This led to the recurring jokes about Iddqd's absence from matches, with players pulling out their phones and pretending to read a message from Iddqd, "Hey guys. I really want to be there to support you in your big match against the Spitfire, but my Uber Eats hasn't arrived, so I won't be able to make it." Because the team got a cut of any signed player's streaming revenues, there was no reason to cut him loose completely, though his teammates could go weeks without seeing him at Blizzard Arena.

CHAPTER 8

A NEW PLAYER HAS ENTERED
THE GAME

In Stage 2 cracks in the Overwatch League started to show. They were caused just as often by external events suddenly foisted upon the league as by the actions of the people within the league. Either way, they created something of a rough patch. The first big challenge was a cultural sensation called *Fortnite*.

Ask any parent about video games in 2018, and *Fortnite* is the first word that will come to mind, the game that even your grandma has heard of. When *Overwatch* was released in May 2016, *Fortnite* didn't exist, nor did it exist when Blizzard announced the formation of OWL in November 2016. By the time Blizzard announced the final teams for the first season of OWL in September 2017, *Fortnite* had introduced the now-famous battle royale format of their game. *Fortnite* was originally a team-based player-versus-environment zombie survival game in which players fought to survive a fortnight in the zombie apocalypse. It didn't make much of a splash until Epic released the battle royale version, a competitor novel player-versus-player first-person-shooter, therefore a direct competitor with *Overwatch*. *Fortnite*'s new format was basically a cartoony rip-off of an existing, wildly popular battle royale game called *PUBG*. The battle royale format popularized by *PUBG* and *Fortnite* was based on a dark Japanese book and movie in which juvenile delinquents are sent to an island, each with a unique weapon that ranges from a fork to an Uzi, and only one survivor is allowed to reintegrate into society. Battle royale games start with players parachuting empty-handed onto an island, where they scramble to find weapons to defeat the other ninety-nine enemies also scrambling around the island. A lethal surrounding storm shrinks gradually around them, forcing the players closer together to stay in the eye of the storm. *Fortnite* was the perfect combination of novel premise, cartoony graphics, precise gameplay, and the brilliant idea to include a *Minecraft*-style ability to build structures, which connected with hard-core and casual gamers alike. By the end of Season 1 of the Overwatch League, 125 million people were playing *Fortnite,* and Epic Games, the makers of *Fortnite,* would reportedly earn $3 billion *in profits* in 2018. That was roughly double the profits for all of Activision-Blizzard's business, which included ten different game franchises.

The surprise runaway success of this rival game, while corporations such as Blizzard, sports tycoons like Robert Kraft, and sponsors such as T-Mobile and Toyota were pouring millions into OWL, made for some interesting juxtapositions. A guy like Jack Etienne, who owned a portfolio of teams under Cloud9, could take it in stride. His *Overwatch* team, Spitfire, wasn't even the most important team in his portfolio (that would be the Cloud9 LoL team). When Jack was invited to his daughter's school for take-your-parents-to-school day, he mentioned that Cloud9 had recently signed full-time *Fortnite* streamers. The students jumped up and began emulating the dance moves from the characters in the game. He realized then how much more powerful the fandom would be among this next generation of esports fans being raised on *Fortnite.* He could enjoy that opportunity, while owners of rival esports organizations whose only viable team was in the Overwatch League were left wishing the kids were fans of the right game.

Overwatch League viewership would decline throughout Stage 1 and continue to decline through Stage 2. The official line among those in OWL who would talk to me

inexplicably disappeared from starting rosters, the league risked losing authenticity with its fans, who were fully up to speed on every scandal thanks to the OverwatchTMZ subreddit. This command-and-control approach seemed especially discordant when contrasted to the fun, open, and not-so-serious tone struck by *Fortnite* esports.

In Stage 2, Shock dodged controversy, but they had their own problems to solve—namely, how to come back after a disappointing 3–7 finish in Stage 1. Brett had gotten to work, calling superagent Ryan Morrison, who represented between 60 and 80 percent of the players in the Overwatch League, depending on whom you asked, and told Ryan he was in the market for a new assistant coach. "Ideally someone who speaks Korean." Brett had his eye on a few Korean prospects.

Ryan had the perfect person for him. "He's already interviewing with teams," Ryan said. "He's Korean, he speaks English, and he has a great mind for the game." That man was Jae Choi, better known as JunkBuck, a name he had created based on an untranslatable Korean *Starcraft II* meme, which all the players would learn to enjoy yelling from the practice room.

When *Overwatch* came out, JunkBuck was one of the lucky few invited to beta-test it. He'd literally won the lottery, having submitted his email along with hundreds of thousands of other people hoping to be selected as a tester. He remembered staying up all night the day the beta launched. "When I play a game," he said, "I have to keep going until I get to the end of it. But with *Overwatch*, there was no end. So I would play thirty hours straight, then sleep twelve hours, then play thirty hours." The game had come out just when Junk had returned to live at home after college. He worked part-time driving Uber and as a waiter, though mostly he played *Overwatch*. JunkBuck tried to become a pro player. He hit a 4,400 skill rating in Season 4 of Competitive Play, which meant he was in the top 1 percent of players in North America. When the team he played on blew up, he decided to become a coach for a team called Toronto Esports. It was an online gig that he could do from his bedroom. He didn't tell his parents he was doing it, knowing that they wanted him to get his master's in architecture. Instead, he merely told them that there was something he wanted to do, but he didn't want to say what it was until he had become more stabilized. He didn't tell them it was about video games, though they knew it was something on the computer. Perhaps they figured their son was attempting to launch a career in porn.

While Junk secretly coached Toronto Esports from his bedroom, the owners decided to sell the team to the Boston Uprising. Toronto Esports would become the Boston academy team (like a farm team) in the Contenders Overwatch League, putting Junk in a position to look for a job with an OWL team when that league launched. He had two teams interested: the Houston Outlaws and the San Francisco Shock. And although Houston were then one of the top teams and Shock toward the bottom of the league, Junk was swayed by Andy and Brad, who made it clear how much they wanted him.

The first practice Junk observed after signing on was a mess. Not only was the roster, with players like Super and Sinatraa who couldn't yet compete and others like Nevix playing heroes they had never used before OWL, not built the way he would have done it, but there were constantly guys just talking over each other. Brad would have something he wanted to say; one assistant coach, Harsha, an entirely different observation; and the other assistant coach, Legit, perhaps exclaimed a profanity he couldn't hold in; and all the messages got lost on top of each other. Even worse, the scrims, the building blocks of video-game strategy building and practice, were horribly disorganized. "Players just did whatever they felt like at that moment," Junk said.

JunkBuck would provide more structure to practice and increase the level of feedback that players would receive, filtering out the distortion. His bilingual talents also enabled Shock to start scouting and recruiting Korean players, which they did. But most importantly, he would tell them about a player on his old team who he thought could solve a lot of Shock's problems: Grant Espe, also known as Moth.

JunkBuck's scouting report on Moth was music to Brett's ears: he was possibly the best US Mercy player, with an unbelievable ability to track the opposing team's ultimate charge. Ult charge is based on damage dealt and healing done. To track the opposing team's ult charge, he had to track how much damage each enemy had done to his teammates and how much healing the enemy team had done, which was based on how much damage Shock were doing to them. How on earth could a person track twelve different pieces of data like this? It remains voodoo to me. He appeared to do it entirely in his head, only rarely asking a teammate for a damage or healing update, and he was uncannily accurate. The players couldn't see whether an enemy had their ult ready, but viewers got all the information. I got even more information than a typical viewer, as I sat in the dugout. The dugout was a cozy little room with a couple of coaches and chairs, two computers so subs could warm up, a board on the wall that said, "___ days until last C9," one TV showing the broadcast, one TV showing six different feeds that the coaches watched, and a little speaker that outputted the in-match player comms. This meant that the dugout was always filled with hyperactive chatter of the players onstage during matches, so I could track Moth's tracking accuracy. And he was deadly accurate. Across at least half a dozen matches I watched from the dugout, so I could hear player comms, I never saw him make a mistake when telling his teammates which ults would be online for a coming battle. What was even more astonishing to me was that when a player would ask what percent a particular enemy was toward their ult, Moth would guess within 2 percent of it. Other Overwatch League players shared the ability to track enemy ult status, but it was impossible for anyone to be better than Moth. He was near perfect.

The problem at that moment was that Moth was owned by Robert Kraft's Boston franchise. The guy running Boston, a former *Starcraft* pro, had developed something of a reputation for being a tough personality. One caster put it this way: "If he wins, he's great. If he isn't winning, he's not nice." Brett had to figure out how to strike a deal for Moth without tipping how much he needed him. Behind the scenes, he went to work.

When JunkBuck accepted the assistant coaching job with Shock, there was no hiding it further: he had to tell his parents about what he was up to. They took the news better than he had expected, and he moved out of his parents' house and into the San Francisco Shock housing and got to work. The first match of Stage 2 for Shock was against the Los Angeles Gladiators. Shock had already lost to them in the ninth match of Stage 1. Since then, Gladiators had acquired a new player, Fissure, the same Fissure who had played on the KongDoo team that Jack Etienne had acquired before the final OGN Apex Series tournament. Fissure was one of the best tanks in the world; he just wasn't quite as good as the other tanks on Spitfire, Fury and Gesture. Given that, he was forced to sit out quite a bit playing for Spitfire during Stage 1, and he was very unhappy about it. Jack for his part wasn't sure what to do. "I had never had this situation," he said, "where I'd had that many players on the bench all fighting for roster spots." Though Cloud9 owned ten other teams, none of the others kept a bench of substitutes.

The fact that Spitfire didn't have transparent systems of best practices in place exacerbated the disgruntlement. There was no clear path for what you needed to do to get on the main roster if you'd been relegated to the bench. Fissure struggled without that structure, so Jack sold him to Gladiators and also sold Rascal to the Dallas Fuel. Rascal's exit line was, "I'd rather be the head of a snake than the tail of a dragon."

Soon, Shock and Gladiators faced off in the second stage, and with Fissure added to Gladiators' lineup, it promised to be a dramatic matchup. Shock tried to play into the spectacle, announcing on their social media accounts before the players walked onto the arena, "It's about to get weird. Grow out your moustaches boys." (Shock had been experimenting with being the weird team in social media messaging, an approach they would later abandon.)

The Shock players emerged from backstage and proceeded down the center aisle of the arena, giving high fives to the fans along the aisles. Dhak did his signature entrance move, curling his arms up by his head and flexing both biceps. One huge Shock fan who drove down from Sacramento (a six-hour drive) for every match of the inaugural season and led the chant, "SHOCK, SHOCK, SHOCK," said his piece, loud enough to startle the small children in the arena.

In the game, Dhak played Lucio. Mercy had been nerfed by Blizzard before Stage 2 started, meaning Dhak would mostly avoid being savaged by the analyst desk for his Mercy play. The analyst praised Dhak for his gameplay as Lucio, but still it wasn't enough. Fissure proved a stunning addition to Gladiators. In analyzing the match, Soe said, "I was at first questioning the pickup of Fissure by Gladiators, because he doesn't speak English. If you think about it, how much do you really need to talk as the tank? It's all short calls of heroes. Everyone should be able to understand that." They clearly had, as the new-look, hometown Gladiators destroyed Shock 4–0.

For a few minutes after the packed match, a rare full house, many fans stayed in their seats, either dazed or celebrating. Some held up their signs, hoping to get one more chance at the camera. One said, "Give Sym Healing Turret," referring to Symmetra, a hero who has the ability to place turrets that deal damage. That sign wasn't about either team—it was a message to Blizzard. Sym was never picked by any pro during the whole season, even though Symmetra had the highest win rate in *Overwatch* casual play (when teams have a Symmetra, they prevail 60 percent of the time). Her turrets were hugely vulnerable to the accurate scope of a pro and didn't do much damage anyway. It had even become a running gag, where players would pretend to opt for Symmetra in the thirty seconds before the match began as a way of teasing the fans. Another sign directed at Blizzard said, "The Mercy Nerf Was an Inside Job," referring to the changes made to Mercy's ultimate ability, while also referencing the online meme "9/11 was an inside job." (The so-called Mercy nerf had taken her pick rate from 97 percent in Stage 1 to 37 percent in Stage 2. It was in fact exactly what had given Dhak new life, as his best character, Lucio, became viable again, his pick rate jumping from 10 percent to 53 percent.) The inside-job meme seemed to be popular primarily among people too young to remember living through 9/11.

Inside Shock's practice room after the game, the players were glum, and for the first time you could smell the defeat in the air. "We didn't lose to Gladiators, we lost to Fissure," Babybay said. "That kid fucking carried." Babybay knew about carrying his team. He'd felt pressured to carry Shock during Stage 1 as the primary damage and had ranked first in damage dealt among all OWL players. Babybay was humble about this accomplishment. He said that raw damage output isn't a good stat, as he could just be "shooting fat," meaning shooting tanks while they're continuously healed. Paradoxically, dealing a lot of damage to enemies can actually hurt your team's chances of victory, because if you're shooting fat, then you're letting the enemy healers build ult charge but not scoring any kills. Babybay was similarly humble when I asked how he felt about being considered a tracking god. "Yeah, not like Dafran, though," he said. "Dafran's on another level."

Brad stood in the corner, arms crossed, giving the players a chance to recap. When asked about the game, he pinned the loss on poor communication. "Ours fell apart," he said. Overwhelmed in the face of a tough opponent, Shock stopped playing as a team. Brad glanced occasionally at the boys, as if wanting to stay attuned to what they were saying to each other.

Most of the guys were quiet by then and scanning Twitter with unbelievable speed. Could they possibly be reading that fast? Some of them watched Twitch streams, a few of them VODs (VOD stands for video on demand; it just means a recording of the match). Sleepy started playing a game in which small numbered circles appeared on the screen. The first few appeared slowly, then they appeared faster and faster still, and you had to click them as quickly and as close to their center as possible. It was a game designed to improve reflexes.

Nate Nanzer came in, surrounded by men in suits who looked like they might be potential team owners for next season. "Each team has their own practice room," he said to the suits. "This one is above average from a cleanliness perspective." His perfect delivery of this line caused me to laugh out loud. None of the suits laughed; they just nodded their heads and moved on. Nate planned to keep expanding the league until there were twenty-eight total teams.

Brad gathered the guys around, and they sauntered into a circle like they had done it a thousand times before. "Danteh," he said, "your calls were really good. To targets, to locations. Clarity of calls was good."

"Preplanning is still weak, though," JunkBuck said. "We don't know the intention of their attack." He seemed to be alluding to the lack of ability of the team to track ults, which meant they couldn't predict how the other team would approach a given team fight. Junk told Dhak, "You have to listen to Babybay's call."

Dhak raised both palms in the air. "I wasn't even close. What do you want me to do?"

JunkBuck sat down to look at the call in question more closely, a point in the match when Babybay wanted to push onto the point. "Yeah, Nevix could have helped," Junk said. He started capturing little clips of the VOD at alarming speed, then provided play-by-play feedback to Dhak and Babybay. Dhak pushed back on his comments. "No. You should sprint *here*," Dhak said as he pointed to the map.

"When monkey's ulting?" Junk said, apparently rhetorically.

"Every single comp, you go high ground," Dhak said, his pitch rising. "Not on Widow! You know that I have you on that one."

"Okay, yeah," Junk conceded. "On Widow, ground is right." They were analyzing the correct decisions to make in one particular area of a map, against a particular enemy team comp, in a particular situation. The granularity at which they examined their gameplay was not dry or boring to them. They were deeply invested in the minutiae.

Soon, the talk was over and they started a scrim. In addition to the usual accusations that a composition was broken, they said things like, "That's all that Boston did. I don't know how we didn't realize that." "Philly ran it yesterday."

The scrim ended, and as the guys were starting to get ready to leave, Sinatraa watched a video of the rapper Lil Pump throwing handfuls of weed into the audience at his show. "What a life," he said.

Other guys gathered to provide commentary. Eventually, a debate arose over who was more mature, Lil Pump or Justin Bieber. Still, none of them had their heart in it.

The players wanted to keep the atmosphere light, but they were clearly beaten down.

Each would handle the increasing stress of continuing to struggle in OWL—and watch dreams of the $1 million prize slip away—differently. Dhak would spend that night "staying loose," as he put it. Babybay would practice with training bots, programs created to hone your aim and reaction speed. Sleepy was going to play his game with the circles, and Nevix, who played tank, was going to practice Widowmaker headshots. An odd choice, except that Nevix had taken on the tank role out of necessity: he was signed to Shock as a damage player, despite the fact that there was only one tank on the roster old enough to play, Nomy. So Nevix set aside his two years of grind on damage heroes and learned to play D.Va. Nomy was going to watch the Gladiators' VOD and eat dinner. Danteh would play a custom *Overwatch* match. And Sinatraa had an ambitious schedule ahead of him, he boasted, composed primarily of watching Lil Pump videos.

Shock lost their next two matches: the first to Seoul Dynasty, the team owned by Kevin Chou, who had originally wanted to buy San Francisco's team, and the second to Noah's Los Angeles Valiant. With those defeats, it seemed that the future of the team was in doubt. Even beating the hapless Shanghai Dragons, which sent the

Dragons to 0–14 on the season, couldn't bring much solace to the players or their disappointed fans.

One of Shock's final games of the second stage was notable for one of the players on the opposing team—xQc, the player who had been suspended by OWL for his homophobic comment on his Twitch stream directed at Muma. He had served his suspension and now rejoined with the Dallas Fuel. Many were eager to see how xQc, one of the best-known players, would fare back in the league.

He didn't perform. Danteh, Dhak, and Nevix played extremely well, and Sleepy won the player of the match. Nomy outplayed xQc on Winston. Shock won 3–0. It would be xQc's last match in the Overwatch League.

For OWL, which no doubt considered xQc a liability, his poor gameplay must have been a relief. The league handed him his second suspension almost immediately after the Shock match based on a controversy he'd sparked the week before: while watching an OWL match on his Twitch stream (meaning his fans were watching him watch a match), xQc had spammed the chat section of the OWL broadcast with a Twitch emote, a little emoticon custom to Twitch, that was an homage to a black "speed runner" (players who try to beat games in record times), whenever Malik Forté, the main host of OWL who introduces the teams, interviews players and fans, and hypes the crowd, and who's African American, appeared on screen. Though it took them a week to get around to it, during which xQc played his last-ever match against Shock, Blizzard suspended xQc four games and fined him $4,000, saying, "xQc repeatedly used an emote in a racially disparaging manner on the league's stream and on social media, and used disparaging language against Overwatch League casters and fellow players on social media and on his personal stream." But xQc failed to show contrition, and a few days later Dallas dropped him. He would never return to OWL.

Shock went back to the drawing board, examining how they could retool. The pressure was on Brett to figure out how to pry Moth away from Boston. Because Moth was on Boston's academy team, any OWL team could offer him a contract, which Moth was free to sign. There was one catch: Boston had the right to match the offer and sign Moth to their OWL roster, instead. Brett thought that Boston was happy with their healers, so they might not want to sign Moth. He couldn't be sure, though. More intriguingly, based on the roster of total unknowns that Boston had signed, Brett suspected that Boston's GM was operating on a tight budget and that the Krafts might have imposed a salary cap. Brett did his best to estimate the suspected salary budget and suggested to Andy that they offer $10,000 more. Andy agreed, they made the offer, and

Boston declined to match. Moth, and his crucial ult tracking ability, could be what they needed.

Dhak, who was benched as a result of Moth's addition, spoke admiringly about the young player's skill and extraordinary potential. "I do think Moth is a better fit for the team right now," he said, "because what this team lacks is awareness. Ever since I got benched, I look at Moth, thinking, 'What is he doing better than me?' Ult tracking is one—there, he's a hundred times better than me." He added that Moth's Lucio was less impressive, still with room to grow. Dhak was the kind of circumspect team player who was still of high value to the team on the bench. Unlike Iddqd, Dhak didn't dream of missing an opportunity to help his teammates in practice or buck them up with his infectiously positive attitude in the dugout. He could still help them—specifically, he could help Moth learn to play Lucio.

In Moth's first Overwatch League match, against the London Spitfire, he died twenty-eight times. His Spitfire support counterpart, Closer, died only thirteen times. Losing a support player early in the fight is the surest path to losing that fight. The constant healing makes a huge difference. As every team fight started, Profit, Spitfire's Tracer player, would pick off Moth. It wasn't pretty, and Shock lost 1–3.

Two matches later, Sinatraa, at eighteen years and three

days old, would finally get onstage. The match was against the second-worst team in the league, the Florida Mayhem, who had won only three of their eighteen matches so far that season. Of course, Shock had won only six of their eighteen matches, but now they had their $150,000 man in the lineup. Sinatraa played his iconic Tracer and Zarya. His Zarya play often awed the audience and casters alike and broke Mayhem's rhythm multiple times. His performance as Tracer was less impressive. Although he outplayed the opposing team's Tracer, they were fairly evenly matched. What should have been the most exciting point of the season was instead the low point, as Shock lost to Mayhem 2–3 in a tight match.

"I played bad," Sinatraa said of the game. "I was nervous. I don't know why. I've played on bigger stages." Earlier that week, an NBC camera crew had followed Sinatraa around all day on his birthday. They'd seen his $150,000 salary posted on ESPN, and they wanted to film him re-signing the contract, which until then had been basically a handshake agreement (any contract signed by a minor can be broken when they turn eighteen). Sinatraa, who'd left home at sixteen and spent the next year and a half living in Atlanta and then Burbank with mostly strangers, spent his eighteenth birthday being followed around by a camera, a boom mike, and a reporter. Perhaps he had more reason than most to suffer from stage jitters.

CHAPTER 9

A GAME THAT HURTS THEM

If Shock had proved a disappointment so far that season—
and according to everyone on the team, they had—the
third stage marked the moment that they turned it all
around and it seemed anything was possible. After going
a dismal 6–14 in the first two stages, they found their
rhythm, defeating the Los Angeles Gladiators and then
shutting out the Seoul Dynasty 4–0.

Part of their transformed fortunes seemed to be the
direct result of Sinatraa and Super, who, having finally
reached the league-mandated minimum age of eighteen,
had begun playing for Shock, though surprisingly it was
Super who provided the boost. Sinatraa had shaken off his
rough start, but his stats on Tracer were league average.

Half a dozen players paid half as much as he was were outplaying him. Individual talent is secondary to team chemistry anyway, and the players had also begun to anticipate each other's movements more quickly than they ever had, moving through the maps in coordinated patterns that revealed the teamwork they had honed over so many months of living together.

After a few more close matches, many of them against the top teams in the league, they had achieved a 4–3 record for the stage, their best yet, and were set to face the formidable London Spitfire in a much anticipated showdown. It was what many considered the "team to beat" pitted against the "team to watch." And, though Spitfire had taken both prior matches against Shock 3–1, this one promised to be different.

As Shock ascended, Spitfire found themselves in the midst of their worst challenges yet. Behind the scenes, the Spitfire players had begun to bristle toward the end of Stage 2 at their head coach, Bishop, who wouldn't allow them to live together in a house, probably fearing that the social aspects of a dorm-like house of young men would serve as a distraction and disrupt their practicing schedules. A "stern coach" in Jack's words, Bishop wanted them to live in apartments, and when he wanted something he got his way.

Yet there was more to the story. The team's general

manager, Chang-geun "Changgoon" Park, whom everyone referred to as Chang, was caught doing something that Jack would only describe as "some really bad shit." Chang apologized to Jack in tears, but Jack considered it a firing offense. It was at this time, with the team in chaos and losing matches and the general manager gone rogue, that the head coach, Bishop, demanded a raise—or else he'd quit. Jack fired him on the spot. He decided to give Chang a second chance and promoted him to head coach, but Chang had never been a coach of any kind, and his primary qualification was his good relationships with Spitfire's star players. Accounting for this, Jack brought back a former assistant coach named Agape, who had impressed him with his knowledge, work ethic, and strong ideas about strategy, the latter of which had caused Bishop to send him back to Korea before the season even started. After that, Jack moved the players to the team house they had long asked for and hired a new general manager, Susie Kim, to help resuscitate the team's morale.

Susie was not who many envisioned would lead what was one of the most prominent Overwatch teams, in part because she was a woman, a rarity in the world of gaming, but also because of her friendly disposition in a world in which (not unrelated to the lack of gender balance) machismo and aggression ruled the day. The first time Susie entered the team house, which was teeming with dark wood furniture and lined with light stone floors (a style I came to think of as Florida baroque), she came bearing gifts: candies and lip balms that had each of the player's gamertags on them.

Lip balms? I had to ask.

"Because I know that all boys' lips are chapped. And because we're in California, where it's so dry, it's even worse."

The players and Susie bonded quickly, and she got a feel for how to work with each of them and the way the different relationships operated.

Profit, a cold-blooded killer in *Overwatch*, was in Susie's eyes "the epitome of everything tiny and adorable." He was the most impossibly skinny person I'd ever seen, not appearing to have shoulders. His wrists were so thin that I found myself wondering whether he had only one wrist bone where movement of the hand normally required two. "Profit is a child," Susie said, not unkindly. "Mentally, he's like twelve." She meant this in the childlike innocence sense. Profit was pure spirit and one of the most lethal Tracer players in the league. "If all of his *hyungs* are happy, he's happy," she said, using a Korean word for his friends who are like big brothers. Profit was a butterfly riding the emotional atmosphere of the team. "It's not about the fame or the money for him," Susie said. "It's about playing good games with friends." He would finish the season with one of the highest kill/death ratios in the league.

Susie quickly found that Cloud9's other star, Birdring, was very introverted and somewhat fragile. For all of Stage 3, his wrist had been hurting, and according to Susie it had affected his attitude. "The whole time I was thinking, 'God I hope I don't have teenagers one day,'" she said.

Birdring's delicacy boiled over on his birthday, when the team's chef made him a traditional birthday meal. "In Korea, you're supposed to have *miyeok-guk*," Susie explained, "which is like a seaweed soup." So the chef cooked it for Birdring, and Susie got him a cake. But when she tried to get him to come down and celebrate with the team, he shook his head. "He's like, 'I refuse to eat with you,'" Susie said. Instead, he bought himself McDonald's and ate it in his room behind his locked door.

In the end, Susie brought the cake and the whole team to his room, and they sang Birdring "Happy Birthday" while he sat in his bed with the covers up. He got up, blew out the candles, left the room, and then walked all the way down to the PC room in the basement. The rest of the team enjoyed the cake together.

Susie found Fury, the youngest on the team, to be a gamer who took charge. "He brought gifts for me," Susie said. She figured he could be the key to turning Spitfire's disintegrating teamwork around.

Gesture, the captain, Susie quickly learned, was a sweetheart. "He wants to make sure everyone is comfortable,"

she said. "Right now, he's going through a quarter-life crisis. When we were losing, he started losing his identity.
He'd always been the best. And then when that status fell
away, he questioned why he was in America, so far from
his family." Not to mention pursuing a career that most
thought was impractical, if not insane. I also became a fan
of Gesture immediately. The first time I met him, in the
dugout before a huge match, he was surrounded by his
teammates, who pounded him on the back as he chanted
a song in Korean while keeping rhythm on his own chest.
It was like a Korean version of the scene in *The Wolf of
Wall Street* when Matthew McConaughey similarly chants
and pounds on his chest in a restaurant, which was fitting
because Gesture had a laid-back confidence and a touch of
drawl to his voice that called McConaughey to mind.

Bdosin, the last player Susie met, was loud, boisterous,
and confident, the team's best trash talker as well as its
worst offender when it came to profanity. Sometimes, his
teammates found his chatter humorous, but other times it
alienated them. "You f***ing piece of trash, why would
you sit there?" wasn't exactly what everyone wanted to be
asked several times a day when they tried to do their job.
There were two sides to the coin though, and his passion
leading the team during matches was audible. Bdosin was
the only player I heard on comms who sounded like he was
actually in a life-or-death fight when he played, shouting

in despair or victory after every team fight and forcefully embracing all of his teammates after wins.

Even with the players now living together as they wished and Susie putting a focus on managing their relationships, these kinds of tensions among the players led to bad results. Before their showdown against the resurgent Shock, Spitfire had gone 3–4 in Stage 3—their worst performance yet after going 7–3 and 8–2 in the first two stages. The team was also suffering from Birdring's wrist injury, whose self-induced nature had done nothing to help their morale: Birdring had injured himself playing a game called *Getting Over It* that involved trying to get a man in a cast-iron cauldron up a mountain using a hammer. By the creator's own admission, the game had been designed to frustrate those who dared to play it: "Why did I make this? ... I created this game for a certain type of person. To hurt them." Clearly, it had gotten the better of Birdring, who, after one particular attempt to beat the game was foiled, slammed his hand down in frustration, spraining his wrist.

The pressure was on for Spitfire to show Shock that they were still on top.

But with Sinatraa and Super now able to play against Spitfire for the first time, Shock had their best chance yet to prevail. Thanks to the addition of the Korean-speaking JunkBuck, Brett was also able to sign an eighteen-year-old

Korean damage named Architect, rounding out Shock's roster.

In Shock's practice room before the match, Nomy, now on the bench with Super in the lineup, showed me *his* wrist brace. (Wrist injuries, I came to learn, were quite common among the players, some of whose joints seemed strained by the hours of daily practice several decades before most people even think about joint issues.) "These things knock you out for months," he said. But because Nomy had already been on the bench prior to his injury, his injury didn't seem to affect the team's demeanor the way Birdring's did to Spitfire's. One of the other players in the room looked up from his computer to tease Nomy for being a frail old man. At twenty-seven, he was among the oldest in OWL, just a year younger than Dhak, who held the official Old Man title.

Soon, an argument erupted over girlfriends—not anyone's girlfriend in particular but just the notion of a romantic partner, which was foreign to the players but which some were willing to defend. It ended when one of the players compared girlfriends to Dementors, the monsters in Harry Potter: "They suck your souls out." With apparently no one around to disagree, the conversation turned to the league commissioner, Nate Nanzer, whom a few of the players claimed to have seen doing karaoke.

One of the bench players scoffed, unconvinced. "Oh yeah, what did he do?"

"I can't tell you," Nomy said. "I don't want to get fined."

As they made their way to the dugout, the minutes counting down until they faced Spitfire, Sleepy asked whether anyone remembered when Sinatraa said the forbidden word during an interview. The other players nodded.

The forbidden word was DreamKazper, a damage player for the Boston Uprising who had been banned from the league two weeks earlier for sexting with a fourteen-year-old girl. She had posted a public Google doc online, writing, "I am Lily, I am 14 years old and in 9th grade. I was taken advantage of by a 21-year-old player for the Overwatch League. He abused his power as a player to coerce me into sending him nude pictures and engaging in explicit facetime activities." She said that she sent two explicit images to DreamKazper through Snapchat, and "on Facetime everything was exposed." If this allegation were true, then DreamKazper possessed explicit images of a minor, in other words, child pornography. Though she didn't have the Snapchat images (Snapchat images disappear) or a recording of the videos, she posted screen grabs on Imgur that appeared to be text exchanges between her and DreamKazper. One of the texts that appeared to be written by DreamKazper acknowledged he knew that Lily was underage, and many of the texts were wildly inappropriate given that knowledge, though the offense, surprisingly, carried only a misdemeanor penalty in California (harmful matter sent with the intent to seduce a minor). After that, the league shut down any mention of Dream-Kazper. In Uprising's next match, though he had been replaced in the starting lineup, the casters were forbidden to mention him. The same word went down to all teams: DreamKazper was verboten.

Many of the casters thought that the scandal was handled tremendously awkwardly. Unable to reference what had happened, they found themselves saying things like, "Boston's doing really well despite...despite nothing they're doing really great." According to nearly every caster and analyst I spoke with, usually many drinks deep, this was a regular source of tension between the esports talent and the traditional sports production people in charge. Ignoring issues just because they were controversial was anathema to esports casters, though there was some trepidation of running afoul of the head honchos and risking not getting their contracts renewed. Well, trepidation for all but MonteCristo. MonteCristo had been brought into OWL even before the traditional sports people, and he spoke his mind about whatever he thought was important. That was just part of the deal in hiring him. MonteCristo had the confidence of someone who knew he could do anything: he just happened to be an OWL caster right now. His willingness to voice unpopular truths regularly earned him ire from fans, and he didn't shy away from pointing out the truth of his predictions when they proved right.

And they were nearly always right. MonteCristo spent an insane amount of time analyzing *Overwatch* tape, which gave him the type of insight into the game usually reserved for OWL coaches. If you have dreams of becoming an esports analyst, you better start grinding that tape.

Even one of the casters could spark a minor controversy. On International Women's Day, Soe, a desk analyst who also conducted post-match interviews (she'd conducted the Muma "rolled and smoked my doggies" interview), posted a tweet in which she thanked men who supported women and had always treated women as equals. This turned Soe into an international feminist talking point. Many were upset, accusing her of making the only day of the year about women about men. She got thousands of replies along those lines but also many from women accusing her of backward misogyny, telling her that she didn't deserve to be part of their gender, and, of course, this being Twitter, there were death threats. The story went so viral that it even made it into Soe's hometown newspaper in Switzerland.

She seemed more confused, even bemused, than upset

when she recounted the story to me. Soe was tough as nails, her story straight out of a Dickens novel: from the age of two she was raised in a Swiss orphanage, a huge converted monastery that she confirmed was drafty. She and her brother would spend weekends with their grandparents or their mother, initially preferring their grandparents for the food, though that would change after they convinced her mother's caretaker (due to health issues) that she needed a computer so that she could connect with the world. That wasn't the reason for the computer: Soe and her brother wanted to play *Quake*. The government-issued equipment proved inadequate to the task, necessitating a series of creative schemes by which two orphans—without a franc to their names—acquired a graphics processor, CPU, and motherboard capable of running *Quake*. Soe had found her passion. She initially became a pro gamer in *Quake* and its sequels, eventually switching to the production side when she realized she didn't have the innate abilities necessary for the highest level of competition. If she couldn't play with the best, she could at least analyze them.

By the time she joined the OWL production team, Soe had been working in the male-dominated gaming industry for fifteen years. She'd had much worse thrown at her than anything from feminists on Twitter, as women in gaming, particularly attractive women, operated under a microscope. If she made one mistake analyzing a match, she had to rebuild her reputation from scratch, while the mistakes of male analysts were no big deal. Because of her good looks, producers were constantly trying to force her into an on-camera, content-light role (her term for this: "tits on legs") instead of her preferred spot at the analyst desk. She'd won that battle, but even some of the comments from fans who admired not just her talents as an analyst (which demanded respect) showed the added layer of scrutiny from being a woman in this world. Many of the players thought of her as the benchmark against which to measure suitors. Babybay once bragged to me that he was going on a date with a girl who was "even hotter than Soe."

In the wake of the scandal, she had been moved off the analyst desk, becoming a sort of team insider who would try to pry secrets out of OWL coaches and managers before matches. It was obvious from the interviews that this was a nearly impossible job, as most of the coaches tried to say as little as possible, reveal nothing of interest, and end the interview as quickly as they could without being blatantly rude.

It wasn't all grim scandal during Stage 3, though, especially for the fans, who continued to show up to Blizzard Arena, keeping it at least half full for most teams and packing the house for both LA-based teams and, surprisingly, the winless Shanghai Dragons. At 0–20 to start Stage 3, the Dragons had more than just an underdog narrative: they fielded a starting roster that now included the league's first woman, Se-yeon Kim, who went by the gamertag Geguri. Geguri, a pro gamer from South Korea, piloted the hero D.Va, a giant pink mech piloted by a pro gamer in South Korea. Geguri had endured the typical additional scrutiny applied to women in gaming. A few Overwatch pros on a South Korean team called Dizziness accused Geguri of cheating by using an aimbot (a type of software hack plaguing online gaming that snaps the player's crosshairs to enemy heads when they get close). If she could prove that she wasn't cheating, they said they would apologize and retire from professional *Overwatch* play. Blizzard came out in Geguri's defense, clearing her name, but Geguri wanted to play on a neutral computer to prove her skill was real.

It was. Three of the players issued apologies and retired, and the team manager pinned the blame on those three in an attempt to clear the other three of wrongdoing. Those three had now found their way into OWL: two were on NYXL, and one was on Seoul. The NYXL players appeared to be truly blameless, but the Seoul player, Xepher, admitted that he was complicit in an apology to Geguri he posted on Inven (a website that's sort of a mix of IGN and reddit). Geguri didn't hold a grudge, saying of Xepher on her Twitch stream, "He never did anything to personally harm me.... It's all in the past, and I don't have any ill feelings towards him.... Since we're both in the OWL and play the same position, I think we'll just motivate each other. I really don't have any ill feelings, you know?" Geguri became an instant hit with fans, as much for her positive demeanor and frog-based Twitter stream as because she was the first woman in OWL. Unfortunately, she wouldn't be able to turn Dragons around. The team was just too dysfunctional. But at least Dragons now got to play home matches to packed crowds, even if they continued to lose every time.

There were also fun and silly moments in Stage 3. Fans noticed that after the players high-fived them on their way up to the stage, they would wait until a page had run out from backstage to give them a squirt of hand sanitizer to touch their equipment. The next match, as soon as the last player sat down onstage, the crowd chanted in unison "sanitiiiiize, sanitiiiize," while rubbing their hands together. They'd coordinated among themselves between matches. This meme went everywhere, the players getting into it, the fans cheering for the previously anonymous page, and casters working hand sanitizer into their match analysis.

And so, after the Shock and the Spitfire players were introduced for their third match of the season, the audience roared in anticipation of the match, followed by a chant of "sanitize, sanitize, sanitize" to kick off the match.

As it turned out, the match was not at all close. Spitfire crushed Shock 4–0, with every individual player on Spitfire outperforming his counterpart on Shock—Profit ran circles around Sinatraa on Tracer, and Gesture crushed Super on Winston. As soon as it began, the match seemed to be over. The two teams' reversal of fortunes that had marked Stage 3 had utterly failed to translate to their head-to-head match.

After the match, the Shock retreated silently to their practice room, eyes down, energy ground to dust. Ten minutes of muted conversation passed in the room—the longest I had seen the players go without teasing each other. Sleepy had a crease in his forehead I'd never noticed before.

Brad, sitting in a desk chair in the middle of the room, asked the players to gather around him. No one responded. Eventually, he just turned back to his computer and loaded up the VOD, watching the match over all the way from the start, wincing each time a bullet connected with one of his players, as if it had drawn blood.

CHAPTER 10

TRY TURNING IT ON AND OFF AGAIN

Hey, can you come by?" Brett asked. He was on the phone with Brad, standing in the kitchen of the apartment complex where he, Brad, and the team lived. When Brad arrived at Brett's apartment, he entered without knocking. Having lived steps from each other for more than a year now, Shock had achieved a casual vibe, treating each other like family. Brett was finishing a cigarette on the patio, so Brad joined him outside.

"Hey man," Brad said, "what's up?"

Brett took a final drag and ground the cigarette out under his boot. He squared up with Brad.

"Look, we're releasing you."

Brad stood silent. Though Shock had destroyed their chances at the playoffs in the first half of the third stage, they had closed that stage by winning five of their last seven matches. They'd finished the stage with a 6–4 record. In fact, they missed the Stage 3 playoffs only because they had a worse map differential than Gladiators, the tie-breaker when two teams shared the same record. With Super and Sinatraa finally in the lineup and playing well, it seemed it was finally coming together.

"Okay," Brad said, and went back to his apartment to tell his wife.

Brett needed to make a plan. He had sent the players to Santa Monica for the day to avoid anyone catching wind of the personnel move, because the new coach they were set to meet the next morning was that very day still coaching his old team in the Stage 3 playoffs. (That team would win in the first round of the playoffs but lose the Stage 3 championship match to the New York Excelsior, who solidified their status as the best team in the Overwatch League.) Including the four games to end Stage 2 and the first playoff game, the new coach of the San Francisco Shock had put together a fifteen-match win streak. It was astonishing that he was even available and even more astonishing that he chose the ninth-place San Francisco Shock as his next team. Six teams had offered him their head coaching job, with one owner literally getting down on his knees to beg him.

The next morning, the players crowded into the practice room, the full twelve-man roster they had assembled as well as the two assistant coaches, Harsha and JunkBuck, and two new, unfamiliar assistant coaches, plus Brett. I glanced at the chairs, realizing by the look a player gave me as I eyed the last one that it was standing room only for me. Sinatraa looked shaken. Dhak looked wary. Sleepy and Moth look uncharacteristically excited. Nevix looked exactly as he always did, solid.

The door opened, and in stepped a Korean man. He wore a solid blue sweatshirt over a T-shirt, sweatpants, and sneakers.

"Hello, my name is Crusty. I'm from Boston Uprising," he said. He spoke with a strong Korean accent, which meant a little trickiness with the *r* and a melodious rising and falling running through the sentences (Korean is a tonal language). He spoke forcefully and with confidence, like the Kool-Aid Man crashing through the language barrier. "I think this team have a great potential," he said, chopping his right hand into his left palm in rhythm with his words. "That's why I choose this team. And I believe in you guys, but I think there's a little problem now." At this, Crusty looked around the room, catching the eye of the players, one by one, seeming to want to confirm, from a look, that each agreed. They did. "I think you guys are doing better and better. I think next stage, you guys can go to title match. My opinion." He looked up and took a step back, like he was finished. Then he raised a finger in the air. "Also, I want to be your friend," he said. "Don't be afraid to talk me. So, let's make the best team, okay." He said okay flatly, like it was a settled matter.

Everyone clapped, and Brett thanked the team for coming in on Monday, their off day, telling them they were free to go. He apologized for the secrecy around the new coach. "I think this is going to be a banger fucking stage," he said. "So let's get it."

For most of the players, that meant back to their computers to check in on social media. There, they found the news was reported. Brett had tweeted it just before bringing Crusty in the door.

I started to sidle up to Sinatraa to get his opinion of the situation and quickly discovered that he didn't want to talk to me or even acknowledge my presence. This was personal for him. He continued to sit in a chair alone, not talking to anyone. It wasn't just that Sinatraa had spent the past eighteen months of his life under Brad's wing, it was that the Stage 3 stats showed that he was a below-average Tracer player in OWL. In what was supposed to be his time to shine, instead another player, Striker, had come off the bench to claim the title of best Tracer in the league. Striker played for Boston, getting a shot to start only after DreamKazper was banned. It was as much due to Striker's electric Tracer play as Crusty's coaching that Boston had gone undefeated in Stage 3. That was supposed to be Sinatraa's story. Instead, he was officially not good, and the coach who'd built the team around him was gone. With a new coach in town with no stake in his recruitment or decision to pay him $150,000, a coach rumored to prefer a whole Korean roster, would he be a starter anymore? And if he wasn't starting, would he even be on the team next year?

Dhak wrinkled his nose as he considered the situation. Moth's face was lit up, so I wondered what he thought. Was Crusty a good coach? "He's one of the two best coaches in the world," Moth said. "Him and Pavane, the NYXL coach." After three stages of play, NYXL were first in the league, with twenty-seven wins out of thirty matches. Boston were second, with twenty-two wins. After going 5–5 in Stage 3, Spitfire were third, with twenty wins. Shock currently had twelve wins. They'd probably need seven wins to make the Stage 4 playoffs. If Crusty could keep his regular-season streak alive for ten more games, Shock had an outside chance of qualifying. Although not a great record, 22–18 could put them in the playoffs if everything broke right.

When Crusty took over, practice changed dramatically. Instead of having desks along each wall, they were arranged into pods. Navigating the practice room suddenly became a game of shimmying between desks roughly six inches apart. The lights were kept off far more often, meaning the only light came from computer screens or the big-screen TV on the wall. Crusty would play VODs on the TV, and then he would use Microsoft Paint to draw on his computer. For instance, he would replay a clip of the team attempting to take a point called "Shrine" on the map Nepal and showed the players how he wanted each of them positioned: using the two sets of columns on the map to protect the healers from opposing fire. Then, when the opposing team decided to come down the stairs to pounce on the healers, he crudely drew on the map in Microsoft Paint who should move where, so that it became a trap.

Under Crusty, the players began to receive ten-page printouts with notes on the prior day's scrims. The printouts would include images to show when the individual player's positioning was off, how opposing teams tended to group, suggestions for flanking angles, and so on. They were incredibly detailed, and Crusty and his team produced them five days a week. On days off, the coaches—Crusty; an assistant coach he brought with him from Boston, NineK; plus JunkBuck and Harsha, whom Crusty kept on board—would convene, usually at the practice room, to review other teams' VODs, discuss the meta, or plan for the week. Crusty promoted Chris Chung, the team manager of NRG's Contenders team, to team manager of Shock. Chris and Crusty were friends, and the high opinion that Chris held of Andy and Brett had been a factor in Crusty's decision to choose them. Under Chris, schedules were planned much further in advance: no more of the one-day-at-a-time business. Players were encouraged to adopt a more normal sleep schedule. For the first time ever, I heard a coach ask a player what they typically ate on match days. It seemed that, as had happened in football and basketball decades ago and in baseball perhaps around the turn of the century, the professionalization of *Overwatch* had arrived.

Unlike those sports, however, with their years-long processes for changing minor rules, *Overwatch* continued to grapple with the challenges of keeping the game both fresh—by introducing new maps and characters—and balanced—by nerfing and buffing hero abilities—all while managing the fallout that resulted from those changes in a league with millions of dollars of prize money on the line.

Under Crusty, Shock lost their first match, once again to one of their California nemeses, this time the LA Gladiators, led by Fissure. Shock were just the first casualty of Fissure's warpath to the playoffs. After three stages of the play, Gladiators were ranked seventh in the overall standings, out of playoff contention. Led by Fissure's dominant tank play, Gladiators would go 9–1 in Stage 4, making the playoffs as the #4 seed.

Shock then beat the crumbling husk of Seoul Dynasty, the preseason favorite. Seoul, like Spitfire, suffered from too much talent on the roster creating a poor team environment. Ranked first in every preseason power ranking, Seoul finished eighth and missed the playoffs.

In their third match of Stage 4, Shock faced off with their

old friends, Spitfire. Spitfire had won all three matches so far, though Shock now had Crusty. It wouldn't be enough. Spitfire would remain undefeated against Shock in the first season. The score read Jack 4, Brett 1 (and the one, Sinatraa, had so far been a Pyrrhic victory, chewing up a huge amount of salary for below-average play).

Shock then beat both Texas teams, Houston, who'd become an afterthought and would miss the playoffs, and Dallas, who had adopted a strategy similar to a mistake that Brett had already made: signing popular streamers, like xQc and former NRG player Seagull. It didn't work for Dallas either, as they finished tenth.

At 3–2, Shock couldn't afford to drop any wins, and they would play a revenge game against Crusty's former team, the Robert Kraft–owned Boston Uprising. He had left Boston because he thought that he was being micromanaged by the general manager, despite believing that the team's success was due mostly to his hard work. Similar to Brad coaching Selfless, Crusty had recruited unknowns and shaped them into the second-best team in the league after three stages. When Crusty asked the Krafts to give him full team control or release him, they made a bad decision. They let Crusty walk, the equivalent of letting Bill Belichick out onto the free market to keep Rex Ryan in the building, and it immediately blew up in their faces. Boston lost five matches in a row to start Stage 4, and Crusty was determined to deliver the sixth. He was notably agitated the day of the match, the cadence of his speech faster, his English harder to comprehend, as he flew through scenarios he thought his players might encounter from his old team.

After splitting the first two maps, the atmosphere in the dugout at halftime was tense. Crusty told me that the team were making incredibly amateur mistakes, and he was very hard on two of the Korean Shock players at halftime, Architect and Choihyobin. Brett had scouted and recruited Architect and Choi with the help of JunkBuck, and they'd been finding increasing time in the lineup under Crusty. Crusty considered Architect too timid on comms. Architect played Widowmaker, the sniper, meaning he had an excellent view of the field and enemy locations. Yet he never made a peep, as he was extremely shy naturally, which was only exacerbated by having to communicate in a new language. Crusty, whom Brett described to me as the most direct person he'd ever met, couldn't understand Architect's reticence. As Architect stood, eyes wide, cowering under Crusty's instructions for shot calls, Super walked over and put his arm around him, looked at him, and called him "Gosu," a Korean word that literally translates as a "highly skilled person" but is used more like "badass." "He can use Korean. I'll know what he means," Super said to Crusty. "Yeah," Moth chimed in. "Korean's fine. We'll follow your call."

Crusty needed Architect to step up, because he planned

to bench the team's shot caller, Sinatraa. This wasn't due to Sinatraa's gameplay: Crusty believed strongly in optimizing hero compositions based on maps. If he thought a map was more suited to the heroes that Babybay or Architect specialized in, they got the start. It didn't matter who was paid what or who was superior overall. In this way, he really was like Bill Belichick. For this approach to work, though, he needed Architect to assume some of Sinatraa's shot-calling duties. He was clearly nervous as the players headed out to the stage: he couldn't even sit down.

When Architect made his first call to the team, identifying the location of the enemy Widowmaker, everyone in the dugout let out a small cheer. He would continue to shot call, saying more during the next two maps than I'd heard him say in the past two months. Shock would win both, taking the match 3–1, with Super the winning player of the match. Crusty was ecstatic, but that didn't stop him from being a coach. "I feel like we had many problems, and there were many mistakes that, I think you guys know better. But I'm very happy to have the win," Crusty said, breaking out into a broad grin. Now the team could celebrate, pounding Crusty on the back and shouting what had become the team's motto, "Let's get iiiiit."

The team were in high spirits the week after the win, though their mood was dampened when Gladiators notched their twenty-first win, becoming the sixth to do so, which eliminated Shock from the regular-season playoffs and the big money. At 4–2 in Stage 4, they still stood a good chance of making the Stage 4 playoffs if they could win at least three of their last four matches. Their last opponent of the season, the Shanghai Dragons, should be easy enough. Shanghai still hadn't won a match. The other three were a murderers' row of playoff-bound teams: Philadelphia Fusion, New York Excelsior, and the team that had beaten them in the first-ever OWL match, and twice more since then, the LA Valiant. Shock played Fusion immediately after learning they were eliminated from playoff contention, which may explain their flat performance and loss. NYXL appeared to be sandbagging, having locked up the #1 seed a month ago. Still, Shock lost to a sandbagging NYXL team, and for a fourth time to the LA Valiant. In the Season 1 battle of California, the record stood Northern California 1, Southern California 7.

What the team had expected to be an easy win against Shanghai instead turned out to be their highest-pressure match of the season. The Dragons entered the match with a 0–39 record, and this was their last chance to get a win. Blizzard Arena was sold out, and everyone who bought a ticket showed up. The place was packed, and every single person in the audience (besides Tyler, the guy who drove from Sacramento) wanted to see Dragons get a win. "Damn, I really don't want to be the only team to lose to Shanghai," Babybay said before the match.

In a typical *Overwatch* match, the crowd will cheer when

their team definitely win a team battle, which usually means killing at least four of the enemy team. This match was not like that. When Geguri would use D.Va's special ability to eat a Shock ult, the crowd would roar. When any Shock player died, even during a fight they were clearly winning, the fans chanted the player's name who scored the kill. Somehow this environment worked for Shock, or perhaps the Dragons were just that bad, as Shock won 4–0. Although they'd finished a disappointing ninth for the season, they'd at least avoided the ignominy of being the only team to lose to Shanghai.

Crusty would not do better in Stage 4 than Brad had done in Stage 3. Under Crusty, Shock went 5–5 and finished the year 17–23. Some of the players wondered what could have been with better Mercy play in Stage 1 and a dedicated D.Va main that would have allowed Nevix to focus on damage. Talking to everyone in the organization, though, it was clear that the team were confident they had turned a corner. Whether by plan or by complete randomness rationalized as the plan all along, Brett found himself in the enviable position for Season 2 of owning one of the youngest rosters in the league, a team that featured both American and Korean representation and, most importantly, Crusty.

Spitfire managed to limp into the playoffs, going 4–6 in Stage 4. After Jack had fired Bishop, promoted Chang, and hired Agape and Susie, he insisted that the team release their bench players. Jack felt confident that they knew who their best six players were: Profit, Birdring (with a healed wrist), Gesture, Fury, Closer, and Bdosin. Susie pushed to keep NUS on the roster, as she'd noticed that the relationship between the team's healers, Bdosin and Closer, could be volatile. This would prove prescient.

Despite making the playoffs, Spitfire had been in steady decline all season. After winning the Stage 1 playoff (and $100,000), they placed third in the Stage 2 championship (for no money), failed to qualify for the Stage 3 playoff at 5–5, and finished with a losing record in Stage 4. They qualified as the #5 seed with the same record as the #6 seed, Philadelphia Fusion. Both teams had finished the season 24–6, with their best play in the first half of the season, and nobody expected to see either team in the final. The playoff narrative mostly revolved around whether NYXL would choke. There was history behind it, as the same roster that now played for NYXL had previously dominated multiple seasons of OGN's Apex Series before flaming out in the playoffs. NYXL had been sandbagging for a month and hadn't shown anything new in scrims. Maybe they were resting on their laurels?

The rest of the playoff attention focused on the Los Angeles teams: the Stan Kroenke–owned Gladiators, and Noah Whinston's Valiant. Both teams were white hot, finishing Stage 4 with 9–1 records. They'd even played each other, with Valiant winning 3–0. Then Valiant beat the Gladiators in the first round of the Stage 4 playoff and NYXL in the championship match. Despite the #1 seed NYXL's season-long dominance, the recent win over them put the #2 seed Valiant firmly as a favorite to win it all. It was pretty much just those two, with nearly everyone I spoke to expecting a chalk championship, the #1 seed versus the #2 seed, with the only disagreement being whether Valiant could beat NYXL again. The closest thing to an endorsement that Spitfire received was when Monte, commenting on their chances, said, "Well, when they play well, they're basically unbeatable....We just haven't seen them play well in a really long time."

After losing their sixth match in a row to their former coach, Robert Kraft's Boston Uprising won their final four matches to qualify for the playoffs as the #3 seed. Boston had a 73 percent win rate with Crusty and a 40 percent win rate without him. Crusty was very highly regarded among analysts and casters, which was why they believed Boston didn't really stand a chance in the playoffs without him. Plus, DreamKazper had played for Boston. Nobody wanted them to win. They were tainted goods.

The poor play, team turmoil, but most of all the losing record over the last half of the season had taken their toll on the Spitfire players, particularly the hypercompetitive Bdosin. They felt immense pressure to perform in the playoffs, to make Jack believe in them again, to show the world that they were still the unbeatable team that had won the Stage 1 championship.

CHAPTER 11

PLAYOFFS

The inaugural season of Overwatch League was a tale of two seasons for Spitfire. It started off with a bang: they finished Stage 1 with a 7–3 record, qualifying for the Stage 1 playoffs as the 3-seed. They defeated the best team in the Overwatch League, New York Excelsior, in the Stage 1 Championship, taking home $100,000, split evenly among the players and Jack Etienne's Cloud9 (most teams had either 50–50 splits or 60–40 splits in one direction or the other). Spitfire finished Stage 2 with an 8–2 record, again qualifying for the stage playoffs, though they lost to the Philadelphia Fusion in the first round, losing out on the chance for prize money. At the end of Stage 2, with fifteen wins, Spitfire were in second place in the season rankings, behind only New York Excelsior, with eighteen wins. That was when the struggles began—and they were immense. In Stage 3, Spitfire went 5–5, dropping them to third place in the season rankings. In Stage 4, Spitfire went 4–6, dropping them to fifth. The season of the Gladiators, whom they would face in the first round of the playoffs, had taken exactly the opposite course: eighth in the league after stage 1, eighth after Stage 2, and seventh after Stage 3, and then Gladiators passed Spitfire in the season rankings during Stage 4, to finish fourth in the league.

There was quite a bit of history between the teams. On February 20, just before the start of Stage 2, Jack had sold Fissure to the Gladiators because Fissure was unhappy sitting on the Spitfire bench. Spitfire had gone 7–3 (70 percent win rate) with Fissure on the team, though he played only occasionally. The Gladiators were 17–13 (56 percent win rate) since before his arrival, but since acquiring Fissure, the Gladiators catapulted to 21–9 (70 percent win rate). Whatever team Fissure was on was destined, it seemed, to have a 70 percent win rate.

All three of the Spitfire regular-season matches against the Gladiators happened after they sold Fissure, and in all three matches Spitfire lost. Spitfire even lost a preseason match against them. Spitfire may have proven formidable against teams not named Gladiators, but with Fissure in their path they were not even part of the discussion.

*　　*　　*

There were rumblings of trouble in paradise, though. Six teams made the playoffs, leaving only five teams available to scrim against. One of those would be a team's next playoff opponent, and because teams would not typically scrim someone they were preparing to compete against, that left just four pro teams for practicing with, though teams could also scrim against their own academy teams. The four pro teams playing against Gladiators in scrims—New York Excelsior, Boston Uprising, Los Angeles Valiant, and Philadelphia Fusion—saw no sign of Fissure. Instead, during scrims his role was played by iRemiix, the player who had started before Fissure's arrival and since been relegated to the bench.

Teams were confused, wondering whether perhaps Fissure had an undisclosed injury. Others speculated that Fissure was in fact playing, just doing so behind iRemiix's name to confuse the competition. Spitfire realized that without Fissure in the lineup, they might have a chance. Despite the problems in the second half of the season and finishing with a losing record in Stage 4, Spitfire hadn't rolled over just yet. Nobody had seen Gladiators' best player in scrims all week. Maybe things were finally breaking their way.

When the day of the first match arrived, Fissure was nowhere to be found at the arena. Soe wanted to get to the bottom of the situation and discuss it in the pregame analysis, but OWL's production team barred her from mentioning it.

It turned out that Gladiators didn't need Fissure, anyway, as they steamrolled Spitfire, winning the first match 3–0. After losing the first match to Gladiators on a Thursday, Spitfire had Friday to regroup, then they would meet again at Blizzard Arena on Saturday. Spitfire would need to win both matches.

The day following the loss, Spitfire had a practice scrim scheduled against the Philadelphia Gladiators. Within the first twenty minutes of the match, after Bdosin's shot calling continued to lead Spitfire to ruin, his fellow healer, Closer, became frustrated. He wanted to try a different strategy.

"Come on," said Bdosin. "This is gonna work. Let's try it again, let's try it again."

They tried, and failed, two or three times.

"Hey," said Closer, who was sitting to Bdosin's right, "what if we tried my idea instead?"

"Why would we do a f***ing r*tarded thing like that?" said Bdosin.

"Your idea hasn't worked at all," Closer said. "Why is my idea r*tarded?"

"Because you're f***ing r*tarded."

"Why do you have to always talk that way. That's not cool." Closer took his headset off and threw it at his monitor.

Bdosin stood up and shoved Closer.

"What the hell?" said Closer. "How dare you touch me like that?"

As the drama hurtled toward what seemed sure to be a fistfight, the players shouted "PP," slang for "press pause," and the coaches emerged from their dugout in the adjacent basement room, rushed in, and took Bdosin and Closer outside separately to try to calm them down.

Susie had just entered the house with Sideshow, one of the OWL desk analysts, only to nearly collide with Profit as he sprinted from the basement to the top floor. She asked him whether he was alright, knowing he was supposed to be in scrims against Fusion right now. Sideshow had come specifically to watch the scrim, to help him better cast the match against Gladiators the next day.

"The atmosphere's really bad," Profit told her. "Something really bad happened right now. And things are... bad." Profit disappeared upstairs.

Chang flew up the stairs from the basement. "I'm done. I'm done with this," Chang said to Susie. "I can't do it with these kids anymore."

Susie frowned. "What can I do to make this better?"

"I don't know. Maybe take Closer on a walk or something. Can you talk to him? He's really upset."

Then Susie remembered the scrim they were supposed to have been playing. Philadelphia had been left in the dark for forty-five minutes, ever since Spitfire had asked for PP. She checked her phone.

"What the fuck is going on?" the Fusion coach had texted Susie. "Why are you wasting our time?"

She told him that something internally complicated happened, texting, "I'm really, really sorry." She took a deep breath. First things first—should they continue with the scrim?

She went outside, and asked Closer whether he thought he could continue the scrim if they subbed in NUS for Bdosin. Closer said yes.

"We'll continue right now, I promise," Susie told Fusion.

NUS played for Bdosin, who was cooling his heels, smoking cigarettes in the backyard with Jfeel. They had a long talk that ended with Bdosin in tears. "Listen," Jfeel had said, "when you do something stupid, do you ever hear any of the coaches tell you you're r*tarded? This is what it is to be a person of professionalism. We need you to support your teammates, to be their *hyung* the way they see you." *Hyung* means "older brother" and carries with it an obligation to look after the young ones. Bdosin, at age twenty-three, was the oldest player on the team by four years.

Bdosin didn't want the team to suffer because of him. He walked down to the basement as Closer was finishing the scrim.

"I'm really sorry," he said, tear marks still visible on his face. "I shouldn't have said that."

"It's okay," said Closer, "I shouldn't have lost my temper."

"Did you win the scrim?" asked Bdosin, suddenly sporting a huge grin. They'd won the last map. Bdosin and Closer high-fived, and Susie relaxed.

The next day, Saturday, in the morning before Matches 2 and 3 against Gladiators, Coach Chang said to the players, in lieu of a speech, "Why don't we just go out, show them what we got, and go down kicking and screaming?" He glanced around at his players, pensive, then patted a couple of them on the back, and left it at that.

Despite Bdosin and Closer making peace, the team decided to start NUS instead of Closer in the second match. Facing what was likely their last match of the season, Spitfire's gameplay dramatically improved. "They let go of everything and played exactly how they practiced onstage," said Robin, the team manager. "Things started clicking. They played without any sort of expectation." Spitfire played with a carefree, almost fatalistic attitude toward the result of the match for the first time that season.

Bdosin would let out a long battle cry over Spitfire's comms six times that day. Spitfire beat Gladiators 3–0, 3–0, to advance to the semifinal.

*   *   *

Valiant were the meat and potatoes of the Overwatch League. Almost algorithmic, they were derived from a statistical model developed by the owner, Noah Whinston, to identify talent. With a sabermetric eye, he pulled together a team of Giambis and Hattebergs, guys who get on base but don't do anything flashy.

The match was lopsided from the get-go, as Valiant couldn't keep up with the suddenly transcendent play of Spitfire. Spitfire simply had too much individual skill and could feel the rush of energy from the crowd, who began to see that something special was happening. Spitfire were the definitive underdog, with literally everyone picking Valiant to win, but they weren't playing like underdogs. It looked more like six Ted Williamses against six Scott Hattebergs. Spitfire won 3–1 on Wednesday and 3–0 on Friday, punching their ticket to the championship only a week after nearly disintegrating in a fistfight. And they were clearly having the most fun they'd had all season.

After the match, Spitfire's social media manager, Mateus, perhaps best known for his voluptuous hair that reached down to his waist, which he claimed never to have cut in his life, let his emotions get the better of him. If the London Spitfire won the championship, he said, he'd shave his head.

CHAPTER 12

CHAMPIONSHIP

On a Friday afternoon in late July in Brooklyn, there was confusion at the media table in the Barclays Center. Normally the venue for the NBA's Brooklyn Nets, the 19,000-seat arena had first opened to eight Jay-Z shows in a row, with total attendance of 120,000. Tonight, it was hosting the first match of OWL's finals. Inside at the media check-in, despite recognizing me, the public relations crew couldn't find me on their list. I told them that I had something that had been described to me as an "all-access pass," but they had no idea what that was. This made sense, as I actually had no idea what kind of pass I had—or whether I had one at all. I just thought "all-access" sounded right. I refused their compromise offer of a media pass. "I'm supposed to be with the team in the locker room," I said, trying to sound like I really believed this. "Behind the scenes," I added. This didn't seem likely to them, which again made a good deal of sense to me—I never could have imagined I'd find myself in this situation—but they obliged me and started a chain of phone calls and text messages, eventually reaching the general manager of the team in question, the London Spitfire: Susie Kim. The ruling came back, and a young woman began punching holes in a plastic badge that she then just handed to me. "You can't go into the owners' suites or onstage. You can go everywhere else." Hardly able to believe that had actually worked, I moved into the arena in wonder at the strange journey that had brought me here among the journalists and media production teams, descending past checkpoints until I walked alone through the Barclays Center's quiet underbelly.

I found my way to Spitfire's warmup room, which definitely wasn't the same locker room the Brooklyn Nets used: the ceilings were so low that you could count on one hand the number of active NBA players who could stand upright in it. I felt the constant desire to hunch. There were a dozen open lockers along three walls, so perhaps it was for neighborhood basketball, like a youth locker room. That would be appropriate, as most of the people in this room were teenagers. They'd spent ten hours a day for the past ten years in similarly claustrophobic basements and bedrooms—dedicating hours of practice, entertainment, toil, and anguish that had elevated these six teenagers and old man Bdosin above the tens of millions around the world who wished they could be in their shoes. And their shoes were fly: custom Air Jordan high-tops in Spitfire colors. Later, I would poke my head into the opposing team's locker room and discover that Philadelphia got the good locker room, easily three times the size of Spitfire's, with a lounge area and its own bathroom with a shower. Team Spitfire had no lounge area and used the same bathroom that everyone working the event used, which constantly ran out of paper towels, forcing the Spitfire players to dry their hands on their jerseys and sweatpants.

I was confused as to how that locker room decision got made, because Spitfire entered the playoffs with a higher seed—fifth to Fusion's sixth. Perhaps it had to do with Fusion's pull within the OWL organization, as the Comcast-owned Philadelphia Fusion were managed by the scion of the Comcast fortune.

The seven Spitfire players and three coaches crowded around a few different screens sitting on laminate folding tables. Half of them were watching clips of *Overwatch*, most of the rest were browsing message boards or Twitter, while one watched K-pop videos. They seemed remarkably relaxed, given that a million dollars was on the line and

10,000 fans chanting above their heads. They didn't appear to be bothered by the money, the pulse of the crowd, or a physical environment that left a lot to be desired. Perhaps they knew that the part of the event that mattered was purely a digital spectacle, one these young men could perform better than most anyone in the world. When they went onstage, they would do so confident in their power to dazzle the crowd in the arena and the 10.8 million fans watching online with nimble movements on a keyboard and a mouse, the same keyboard and mouse they'd used to play every match at Blizzard Arena.

It turned out, though, that the main reason the players looked so relaxed was that they were dead tired.

It'd been a rough week. The team flew from Los Angeles to New York in the early-morning hours on Monday. Pro gamers not being morning people, that was already enough to put the week on tilt. Then on Tuesday, two players on Fusion discovered a dead body in the hotel. They didn't know it was a dead body; they just followed a horrible smell. After rounding a corner in the hallway, they were confronted by a man who appeared to be homeless, camped out in front of a room, who told them to get the hell out of his territory. When the front desk investigated, they discovered a body in the room. Despite this incident, both teams stayed at the hotel that night.

The following night, Wednesday, well past midnight, the fire alarm went off for three hours. Spitfire were scheduled to be at a media event early Thursday morning, roughly four hours after the fire alarm was silenced. They showed up late to find that their opponents, the Philadelphia Fusion, had taken all the good seats, spreading out across yellow banquettes, bathed in soft light from the windows while being interviewed by journalists from all over the world. Spitfire assembled in the dark corner that remained, leaning exhaustedly on the cocktail tables, as there were no chairs. They didn't stay long.

Susie, the team's player manager, and the social media manager, Mateus, whose hair was on the line that weekend, left the media event to get some pizza. At the restaurant, the hostess led them to a table on the patio, right next to the entire Fusion team and coaching staff. Fusion noticed them, tensed up, and hushed their teammates. Although it was a beautiful day, the Spitfire managers retreated inside. They were exhausted. Besides the "incident" and the fire alarm, there was a grueling media schedule to generate hype videos for the event. The players trooped around New York saying cruel things about the opposing team in front of famous New York landmarks. During the press conference the prior week, after the semifinal victory over Valiant, a reporter asked the Spitfire players whether they'd ever been to New York. None had. What were their impressions of New York? Blank stares. They whispered to each other in Korean. "They say that they've heard there are yellow taxis," the translator offered.

Now they needed a new hotel, and the managers struggled to solve this dilemma with the few waking brain cells they had left. After listening to them shoot down each other's suggestions—"too expensive," "it would take too long"—I butted in. My brother lived in New York. He had an SUV. I could help ferry all the suitcases for the team into Manhattan.

They jumped at my offer, I think mostly because even a simple logistical problem such as hiring a black car to ferry suitcases sounded overwhelming in their current state. I spent the afternoon shuttling eleven suitcases and one backpack from Brooklyn to Midtown Manhattan. The suitcases were enormous, the hard plastic kind with four wheels on the bottom, but bizarrely light. When I lifted them, I estimated that they were only a quarter packed, at most. I realized for the first time that though every one of these kids had multiple pairs of $1,000 sneakers, they all apparently owned only one suitcase. Moving to America? Their giant rolling suitcase had them covered. Weeklong trip to New York? Giant rolling suitcase. Going on a day hike? Giant rolling suitcase. Although they probably didn't hike. I'd never seen any dirt on their thousand-dollar Balenciagas.

It was my moving services that scored me the invitation backstage for the finals, where, as the minutes until the first match ticked down, the videos of the Fusion trash talk that had been recorded that week in New York started to play on the enormous screen in the arena. After spending the season with champion shit talkers such as Super and Bdosin, the Fusion boasts were tame—and oddly full of hedges.

"Our team's tanks are better because while we have three good tanks," HOTBA said, "they only have two." Beyond being less than damning trash talk, it wasn't entirely true that having three good tank players put Fusion at an advantage. The current meta of the game didn't demand three tanks. The optimal team composition required two, and only two, tanks on the map at any given time, so when Fusion wanted to change tanks, a Fusion player would have to be subbed out, while Gesture or Fusion would simply swap heroes. Fusion carried three tank players, because their best two tank players couldn't play all necessary tank heroes needed for every map and situation.

"I personally believe," HOTBA added, "that the London

Spitfire's weakness is that their damage lineup lacks the ability to carry the game." There was some truth to that— Spitfire's damage gameplay could be undisciplined, mostly based on Birdring's current state of mind and level of wrist pain. But Fusion did have one of the best players in the league, Carpe, who played the hero Widowmaker, the sniper, unlike any other OWL player. He could hit shots from a distance as well as anyone, but he alone would also regularly charge into battle, land four headshots at close range, and single-handedly win the fight for his team. Carpe was the main reason that most seemed to favor Fusion in the championship. His highlight reels were collections of the most unreal plays of the season, but he was also incredibly consistent and an excellent teammate.

Next came Eqo's hype video. He appeared on screen with his arms crossed. "Everything we've done—that's going to be the deciding factor," Eqo said. Does that even mean anything?

Then Carpe appeared on the screen and smiled. "We will be victorious," he said, "because we've always had better teamwork compared to them. They will lose to us again, just like in our previous matches. London's DPS duo is good, but ours are better because we have a bigger hero pool." The fans clapped at this. Eqo was well-known for two things: (1) in the early days of the *Overwatch* competitive Ladder, he'd managed to maintain three different

accounts in the Top 20 of the European Ladder while playing on a laptop from Israel. He said he got something like
twenty-five to twenty-eight FPS, putting him at a severe
disadvantage, and on top of this he had more than a hundred ping (ping is the amount of time it takes for the
server hosting the game to communicate with a player's
computer) due to the distance between the closest European Blizzard server and Israel. Even OWL pros were in
awe of this. (2) Eqo could legitimately play six or seven
heroes at the OWL level. This was known as "having a
wide hero pool" and allowed Fusion to be immensely flex-
ible with their team compositions, even if the rest of the
team were mostly one-tricks.

Next came Spitfire's hype videos, with Bdosin leading
off, saying of Fusion to the crowd of 10,000 people, "I
personally think their strategies are pretty obvious, so it
should be an easy win for us." This got a huge crowd reaction. The Spitfire players were watching the videos from
the far side of the stadium, in a little hallway leading to the
arena floor from their locker room. Bdosin grinned ear to
ear, relishing the sound of 10,000 people echoing the same
noise, the noise that every person seems to make when
they've just witnessed someone get burned: "Oooooooooo."
Spitfire did not let up. "I think Philly had it really easy, for
their path to the playoffs," Gesture said, looking relaxed
and thoughtful. "My thoughts on Fusion's tanks is that

they aren't bad, but at the same time, they don't really stand out either. Fusion doesn't really have anything going for them other than their DPS duo." This last comment elicited laughter and gasps from the audience. Gesture just burned every tank and support on Fusion, and what really made it sting was that he was right.

Profit lacked the conviction of delivery that provided the bite to Bdosin's and Gesture's comments, but he gave it a shot anyway. "London's DPS are better," he said in a chipper tone, "because only Carpe really stands out. Eqo's weakness is that his Brigitte play isn't that good. I have never lost a championship, so we will definitely win the Overwatch League as well." Profit was referencing the fact that his pre-OWL team, GC Busan, had won the final two championships of the Apex Series, taking home $100,000 each time.

Bdosin's closing message was simple: "You guys got here only to be eliminated by us. Good luck!" He said "good luck" the way you say it to someone with zero chance.

The players filed back to the locker room, complimenting each other's videos and imitating the crowd reactions. They were now energized. As soon as they arrived, as if on cue, a page entered the room to tell the team it was time to go onstage.

We arrived behind the stage, where Spitfire and Fusion ascended and waited on stairs at opposite ends. Black-clad tech crews ran around, wide-eyed, hair out of place. This was a much bigger stage than they were used to back in Burbank. The sound from the fans was alive with currents in a different way. A crowd of 450 produces a sound that comes from one direction, over there, but a crowd of 10,000 produces a sound that comes from everywhere, even inside you.

The Philadelphia Fusion players looked stern. Their star, Carpe—the best sniper in the Overwatch League—remained perfectly still, as if he were meditating. The Fusion players all faced toward the stage, standing in a line on exactly six stairs in a row. Spitfire were dancing around all over the stairs and singing K-pop songs to each other. The six Spitfire starters took up ten stairs. Profit, the Tracer player for Spitfire that Susie had described to me as "the epitome of everything tiny and adorable," asked the nearest page whether he could go to the bathroom. Based on the look on her face, it was the furthest thing from possible.

Susie grabbed a water bottle, dumped the water out, and offered it to Profit. I started scouting for a private area behind the stage, which wasn't looking promising. There were people everywhere. In a best-case-scenario emergency pee, Profit's entire upper body would be visible to at least thirty people. So I understood why he passed on this opportunity. After Spitfire lost the first map, I couldn't have been the only one wondering whether it might have gone differently if only Profit had peed in the bottle.

MonteCristo, OWL's most prominent voice, set the scene for the viewers, many of whom were tuning in on ESPN or ABC, likely for the first time, as Nate had struck a network TV deal with Disney for the finals. Monte described the two teams about to face off: "Probably the two best DPS duos on the Overwatch League, and both of them helped by Hanzo being such a prominent force in this current meta." The hero Hanzo, who wields a bow, had been buffed just before the playoffs started.

Monte guided the fans through a few of the players to watch, showing Birdring's sniper stats next to Carpe's. Carpe had double Birdring's kills per ten minutes but died slightly more often. "Watch for Birdring to take a lot of long flanks," MonteCristo said, "waiting for teams to engage, and then picking off supports." Birdring played *Overwatch* like it was a chess match.

"Bdosin is arguably the best flex support in the league," Monte added. "The second-best Zenyatta in the league behind JJoNak, but he's also been awesome on Roadhog, on Tracer, on Moira." Speaking of Bdosin's counterpart on Fusion, Monte said, "Boombox is just not at the same level as Bdosin at playing non-Zenyatta heroes, meaning the Fusion will be forced to sub in HOTBA. They don't have the flexibility. I think Bdosin is an MVP candidate if London wins."

The screen showed a replay of Birdring owning Valiant with positioning, demonstrating the point that he approached the game like a chess match.

Finally, the championship was ready to start. The format was best of three matches, and each match was best of five maps, meaning the winner would be decided in as few as six maps or as many as fifteen maps. One match would be played tonight, the second on the following afternoon, and the third, if needed, on Saturday evening.

Fusion came onstage one by one. Five of the Fusion players waved with both hands as they walked out onstage, though Eqo gave a dramatic salute.

Next came Spitfire. Their uniforms—beautiful light blue, almost teal-colored jerseys with the image of the plane that won World War II in the center of the chest, pressed black sweatpants, and most importantly, custom Spitfire Nike Jordans in their colors, one lace orange, the other white—put the more corporate-looking, orangish-yellow Fusion uniforms to shame. And the shoes—not even close. Spitfire showed their distinct individuality as they walked out onto the stage.

NUS waved to the fans. He was a simple man.

Bdosin, again grinning ear to ear, used his hands to pop the Spitfire logo on the front of his jersey off his chest.

Gesture double pointed at himself, then double pointed at the stage. This was his stage.

Profit smiled and waved, looking comfortable and gen-
uinely happy to be there.

Fury executed a spin move and pointed his thumbs at
his jersey number.

Finally, Birdring spread his arms out to the side and
bowed his head. Perhaps this was bird related.

On the first map the objective was to push a cart all the
way to the other side of the map. Fusion pushed their cart
all the way to the end. Spitfire got their cart within inches
of the finish line, only to be beaten back by Fusion at the
last moment. London 0, Philadelphia 1.

On the second map, the objective was to hold two of
three points all the way until 100 percent. Spitfire won
the first team fight at Point A and defended their position all the way to 99 percent, when Fusion pushed them
off. London switched heroes to a Winston/D.Va comp that
Fusion clearly weren't expecting. Spitfire steamrolled them
and took Point A.

Fusion won the first fight at Point B but managed to
hold to only 41 percent. Spitfire pushed them off the point
and held all the way to 100 percent. Spitfire 1, Fusion 1.

On the third map, teams had to first capture territory
to get the cart moving, then push the cart across the map.
Fusion managed to get the cart going but pushed the cart
only about halfway to the goal when Bdosin used his ult,
Transcendence, allowing four Spitfire players to defeat

six Fusion players. In the next battle, Eqo used a rocket-barrage ult, and Gesture immediately tossed a bubble on him. Eqo's rockets exploded in his face, taking him out. Then Gesture single-handedly closed out the round, using his primal rage ult to swat the entire opposing team down a corridor away from the cart. Fusion ran out of time. Spitfire pushed their cart back past Fusion's mark with ease. Spitfire took the lead, 2–1.

On the fourth map, Volskaya Industries, one team would defend two points (A and B), while the other team assaulted. Fusion assaulted first and managed to capture Point A and achieve 57 percent toward Point B. Point B on Volskaya was notoriously difficult to capture, as it was tight quarters, making it a "killbox" for the assaulting team—57 percent was nothing to sneeze at.

It would nearly be enough to win the map. Spitfire ran out of time before they'd captured Point A. The game then initiated an overtime clock, a small wick that burned down rapidly, though it stayed full as long as one Spitfire player was within Point A. This meant that Spitfire needed to simultaneously shoot their weapons, heal their teammates, avoid enemy fire, and make sure that someone was always touching the point to prevent the timer from expiring. It was high stakes, and Spitfire managed it beautifully. They took Point A, with minimal time now to assault Point B.

Once they entered the killbox, the fighting became

more frenetic, the eyes of the crowd darting back and forth like tennis balls volleyed over a net. Birdring sniped NeptuNo, Fusion's Mercy player: the perfect beginning to a team fight. Profit killed Sado. Poko sent D.Va's mech suit into the middle of Spitfire in self-destruct mode, and in the few seconds it took Poko to summon a new mech, Birdring sniped him. Despite dying, Poko's D.Va bomb killed NUS and Bdosin, while HOTBA destroyed Fury's D.Va mech. The rest of Spitfire went down quickly after that.

In the next fight, Birdring killed Carpe, winning the sniper duel; NeptuNo killed Fury; Profit killed Eqo; then Profit killed the just-respawned NeptuNo with an unreal shot, from far across the map. Everyone was dead besides Profit and Birdring, who stood alone on Point B. They made it to 56 percent before Fusion respawned and killed them. Spitfire were only 2 percent away from winning a third map and the first match.

A few battles passed with little gain in advantage.

With only thirty seconds left to capture Point B, Bdosin popped his Zenyatta ult, which poured huge amounts of healing out to nearby teammates, to give his team a chance of survival in the killbox. Pocketed by Bdosin's healing, Spitfire picked off Fusion one by one. Though all the Spitfire players dealt damage, it was Profit, playing Tracer, who finished them off. And he did it systematically. First, Profit killed NeptuNo, meaning one healer was down. The superfans, knowing how battles that begin this way generally end, started getting excited.

Next Profit killed Carpe, Fusion's best player and primary damage dealer. The audience gasped and for just a moment of anticipation, grew quieter than they had at any moment so far in the championship. Profit used Tracer's ult, sticking a pulse bomb on HOTBA, and the crowd erupted. Then Profit killed Sado, and the pitch rose. Only Poko and Eqo remained alive. Finally, Profit took out Poko, stood on Point B for a few seconds, and won the match. The crowd surged, a shriek that continued to escalate as 10,000 people realized what they had just witnessed: the best play of the entire season. In the final battle of the first match, Profit had killed five of the six members of the Philadelphia Fusion—what's called "5K" in gaming circles—and single-handedly won the fight.

Profit's 5K hadn't just won Point B, or won the fourth map, or won the first match, though it did all those things; it also broke the Philadelphia Fusion.

An hour later, Fusion spoke in muted voices at the postgame press conference. Though there remained at least one match to play the next day, theoretically two if Fusion won the afternoon match, it was only a formality. You could tell from the defeated look of Fusion as they answered press questions and the easygoing nature of the Spitfire players when they took their turn that it was over. The London

Spitfire dominated Fusion the next day, winning the Saturday afternoon match 3–0 to become world champions. Profit was named MVP.

Confetti rained down on the stage, coating Profit, Gesture, Birdring, Bdosin, Fury, and NUS, who had donned oversized world champion letter jackets. Nate Nanzer handed the championship trophy to Jack, who carried it everywhere he went for the next hour. He carried it all over the stage as he hugged and high-fived the players, the coaches, the managers, and Susie. Mateus cried uncontrollably, overcome by the surprise of winning but perhaps also by the ways in which the championship would change his life.

Jack carried the trophy out into the crowd to show it to his dad. I overheard him as he shouted over the crowd, "This thing weighs like twenty-five pounds." He smiled so big that he looked like he was in a toothpaste commercial. Eventually, he retreated (trophy still in hand) into the dugout, where the team continued to celebrate, then back to the locker room. Everyone was jubilant, and Jack was intent on ensuring that everyone held the trophy. "Careful, this thing weighs like thirty pounds."

When Jack leaned back, let out a long sigh, and asked the players what they wanted to do next, the answer came quick and strong. "Steak!" Fury shouted. "Steak!" another said. Soon it was a chant: "Steak! Steak! Steak!" A reservation was arranged at Delmonico's, one of Manhattan's most expensive steakhouses.

But before they could go, Jack had one more thing he needed to do. He ran from the locker room, trophy in hand, carrying it around the whole stadium to let fans touch it. Only when a Blizzard rep approached Jack did he finally turn the trophy back over. "This thing weighs at least thirty-five pounds," Jack said.

"Forty pounds, actually," the Blizzard rep replied.

"Ah-ha!" Jack shouted. It *had* been that heavy. As he walked back to the locker room, he realized that he had carried it for so long that he could no longer feel his arm.

The night that Spitfire won the championship, Mateus did not shed a few tears. He cried uncontrollably—from onstage, through the press conference, the Uber ride to Delmonico's, and through the first thirty minutes of dinner. Although I knew a bit about the emotions that had gone into the season, I started to worry.

At dinner, he finally spoke. "Last year, when I was fired by Noah," he said, "I thought my social media career was ruined. I need to thank you so much, Jack, for the opportunity." When Mateus began to break down again, Jack intervened, raising his glass: "First of all, I'd like to thank Noah." The team roared.

For a 120-something-pound teenager, eating forty-four ounces of steak would be quite a feat. But Fury and Profit, each somehow slighter than the other, had no trouble. "That's the fastest I've ever seen Profit eat," Jack remarked. Perhaps it was because, as the players agreed, this was the best food they'd had in North America.

There was a comfort among the players in the restaurant that—for all their cooperation and teamwork over so many months—hadn't existed before that night in the same way: they were easier with each other, more inclined to give a slap on the back, and equally comfortable offering a compliment or lobbing a teasing insult. It did not take long, though, for their banter to revert to a familiar state. They began comparing their Twitter follower counts, circling around the table. They'd all gained thousands of followers since winning the championship.

A discussion began of whether Mateus had to shave his head bald or simply buzz it. Mateus stroked his hair, ponderous. He was only sniffling now.

Outside the restaurant, Jack turned around and peered in the door he had walked out of like it was a portal into another world to which he would never return. "That dinner was $4,200!" he said. He sounded like he was impressed. The man had just won $1 million.

CHAPTER 13

OFFSEASON

In September 2018, in the LoL League that had in some ways foundered as OWL captured the attention of esports fans around the world, Jack's team succeeded as well, advancing to the World Championship, where Cloud9 went on to place third at Worlds, the highest ever for a Western team. A few months later, when Forbes released a list of the most valuable esports companies, Cloud9 was listed first, with a valuation of $310 million. (By then, the team's investors included Valor Equity Partners, whose founder and managing partner also sat on the board of Tesla.) In second place was Andy Dinh's Team SoloMid, with a valuation of $250 million. (At the time, valuations of Overwatch League teams had been rumored to be around $60 million.)

The coronation of esports as big business had been a long time coming. Behind Jack Etienne's Cloud9 experiment and Nate Nanzer's audacious OWL stretched a road of experiments failed, dreams broken, and fortunes lost. When OWL was soliciting owners and preparing to launch in 2015, they had faced legitimate skepticism in light of esports' track record, and a future in which families tuned in every week to watch their favorite video-game players on television—or even bought season tickets to follow them in person—seemed far off. Then, in the hands of Jack, the future had arrived sooner than anyone thought.

At the esports awards in 2018, Blizzard won Publisher of the Year, while the OWL Grand Finals won Live Event of the Year. Jack's Cloud9 won Esports Organization of the Year—Brett was thrilled for them. "Cloud9 just had the best year for an esports organization in *history*," he told me, with their OWL team winning the $1 million OWL championship; their team placing third at Worlds, winning $450,000; their CS: GO team winning the Boston Major of the ELEAGUE (the very league that Brett helped launch during his time at WME) and with that win earned $500,000. The talent surrounding the Overwatch League would also share in the success. Jacob Wolf of ESPN won Esports Journalist of the Year, largely based on his insider scoops on OWL. Evolved Talent Agency, run by esports superagent Ryan Morrison, who represented the majority of the players in the league, won Esports Agency of the Year.

Exactly how good a job Morrison did making OWL a gold mine for players was something many covering the league speculated about. There was rumored to be a soft salary cap of $1.5 million per team in Season 1 ("soft" meaning teams could go over by paying a luxury tax, similar to the practice in Major League Baseball), which would have put a ceiling on player salaries. Nobody would confirm its existence to me; all I could get was "no comment." If it did exist, the secrecy could have related to the fact that the players weren't unionized, which could have caused the US Department of Justice to look at a salary cap unfavorably.

In trying to get teams to shell out big salaries, Morrison was up against the challenge that, with Blizzard owning all the intellectual property to *Overwatch*, players who wanted to play it professionally had no choice but to accept the salaries that OWL doled out. Players of traditional sports leagues such as the NFL, NBA, and MLB whose intellectual property wasn't owned by anyone and could threaten to form their own leagues received about 50 percent of their league's total revenues in salaries. Under the existing structure, OWL players would be lucky to get 20 percent.

With enough money flowing into OWL, Blizzard might

have hoped that perhaps the ratio shared with players wouldn't need to be high, and with their first season's success, the flow of money was indeed brisk. The distribution deal that Nate Nanzer struck with Twitch for the next two seasons would have paid OWL at least $45 million per year. That was income they would make on top of all the sponsorships with bigger brands now, albeit brands whose appeal to a narrow audience of gamers was often obvious— T-Mobile, Intel, HP Omen, Toyota, and yes, Sour Patch Kids. The HP deal was reported by ESPN to have paid $17 million, and the others $10 million each. Ben Fischer of *Sports Business Daily* reported that the league generated $120 million before accounting for revenues from the championship, which included tens of thousands of ticket sales and three new sponsors that had been brought in only for the championship (Spotify, Cheez-It, and Dolby Audio), not to mention that ESPN and ABC became OWL's broadcast partners for the playoffs and the second season. Given the viewership escalators, the Twitch deal was likely much higher than the reported $45 million. Beyond all those millions, there were more outrageous cash grabs that might have left Martin Luther turning over in his grave, including the digital items the league sold online such as the ability for fans to "cheer" teams online, which meant paying Blizzard a dollar to have your support registered on an online meter.

Blizzard would have a lot more to chew on in the second season. With the first season's success, Nate was able to sell eight more franchises: three more in China (Hangzhou, Chengdu, Guangzhou), two more in the United States (Atlanta, Washington, DC), two in Canada (Toronto, Vancouver), and one more in Europe (Paris). Those sold for $30 million, a 50 percent increase over Season 1's entry price.

If you asked the players, everyone would prefer to be better paid, but there were few complaints about Blizzard. For some, the company's drive to make money had enabled guys like Brad Rajani, Sinatraa, Dafran, and Dhak to live out their dreams, and they wanted to stay at the party as long as they could. Others, for whom it hadn't worked out as well, were often still grateful to have had their chance. After the first season, Shock released Dhak, Nomy, and Iddqd. Nomy found his way onto a Contenders team, Montreal Rebellion, still wanting to try his hand at *Overwatch* despite the league's lower salaries. After playing on the Spanish World Cup team, Dhak would fail to find an OWL team for the second season, and became an Apex Legends streamer. Iddqd retired from competitive play to focus on his *Overwatch* stream.

After losing his job coaching with Shock, Brad Rajani joined a Contenders team called Last Night's Leftovers. Under his guidance, they would become the first

Contenders team unaffiliated with an OWL franchise to make the playoffs in Contenders. He would then be hired as the head coach of one of the new OWL teams, the Atlanta Reign. His former assistant coach Harsha left the San Francisco Shock to join an expansion team, the Vancouver Titans. Shock fan Tyler, who drove six hours from Sacramento for every Season 1 match, would lose 110 pounds during the offseason. He cited the Shock players for inspiring him to work out, and meeting his girlfriend, a fellow Shock fan.

The disappointing year would continue for Sinatraa. Though he was picked for the US Overwatch World Cup team, they were upset in the first round by the UK. At the post-match press conference, Sinatraa was fuming, sitting low in his chair with his arms crossed. I asked the team the first question: What happened? Usually when you ask the team a question, the players look at each other silently, waiting for someone else to answer it. This time Sinatraa jumped at the chance to respond. "We didn't even practice for the UK. Like not at all." The team had been looking ahead to the next match against South Korea, who would go on to win their third World Cup Championship in a row. The World Cup doesn't matter much relative to OWL—there's no money in it, just national pride—but the upset still stung, and it was a sour note to end the year.

EPILOGUE: SEASON TWO

The Shock were much more confident going into 2019 than the end of the prior season might suggest. They had an entire offseason under Crusty, and they'd acquired some serious new South Korean talent. Brett had signed Rascal, the former London Spitfire player who had told Jack Etienne that he'd rather be the head of a snake than the tail of a dragon, prompting Jack to release him. Brett had also acquired two young South Korean players—Smurf and Viol2t—who'd never played in OWL. During the offseason, Brett kept a close eye on the dysfunction in Boston, as he smelled opportunity. The rumor was that their star player, Striker, was unhappy and wanted to be traded. VPEsports reported that Boston was letting Striker try out for other teams, then asking for between $200,000 and $300,000—what other teams considered an outrageous amount—to buy his contract. Striker was being held hostage to a team he didn't want to play for, something the team's manager, HuK, denied in a Medium post. Nevertheless, a few months later Brett was able to sign Striker, bringing the number of stars he'd acquired from Boston to three (along with Moth and Crusty).

"I was very confident," said Brett. "I was telling our sponsors, Sennheiser and Netgear, that we're going to be the world champions." When renegotiating a sponsorship deal, confidence in your prospects makes sense, but this was a little insane. Shock had finished better than only three of the twelve teams the prior year. Now they would finish better than nineteen teams?

With the new talent, Shock played extremely well in practice. Sinatraa estimated they won 99 percent of their scrims in the month leading up to the start of the season, though that success didn't translate to Stage 1, where Shock finished 4–3 (OWL reduced the number of matches in Season 2 from forty to twenty-eight, so each stage was cut to seven matches). One of Shock's losses, to the expansion team Vancouver Titans, was easily excusable. Vancouver, with Harsha in the fold as an assistant coach, had signed the entire roster of a Korean team called RunAway, which had been dominating the minor leagues, winning three of four Korean Contenders seasons and basically every notable tournament in 2018. RunAway, now the Vancouver Titans, would finish Stage 1 undefeated and would go on to finish

Season 2 of OWL in first place, winning all but three regular-season matches. What seemed to be the best team in OWL in 2019 had spent 2018 in the minors.

Besides the players on RunAway, one more star player who'd spent the 2018 season out of OWL played onstage at Blizzard Arena for the first time in Season 2: Dafran. He'd spent 2018 streaming, but he'd been coaxed into the league by Brad Rajani. Dafran played for Atlanta, alongside Babybay, whom Brett had traded to Brad. Dafran brought equal amounts of meme-worthy stunts and godlike tracking. He wore number 99 in reference to the hype video that announced *Overwatch* to the world at the 2016 BlizzCon, where Jack sat in the audience watching alongside the Krafts and the Kroenkes. Dafran had vowed to his fans that if he ever made it into OWL, he would be the first pro to play the hero Torbjörn. He did, and despite Torbjörn's questionable utility at the pro level, Atlanta not only won that first match but qualified for the Stage 1 playoffs as the #5 seed (because of the league's expansion, the stage playoffs were expanded to eight teams). Atlanta would get bounced by Philly in the first round, but it was still a great moment. Someone that nobody thought would ever play on the big stage had not only made it there to play in front of his fans, but he played exactly as the Dafran that everyone knew, as interested in entertaining the fans as winning games. For some hard-core fans, Dafran joining OWL and making the stage playoffs was one of the highlights of the season.

For Dafran, it was apparently enough. He retired from the league after Stage 1, posting on TwitLonger, "I am leaving the OWL and going back to comfy streamer life. Hey, at least we are leaving maturely and gracefully after finishing stage 1, unlike the [anime porn] Selfless incident. I would rather be a streamer at this point in life and chill. I will remember this for the rest of my life with no regret and I can't thank [Brad] enough for pushing me forward to try it out."

Shock also qualified for the Stage 1 playoff as the sixth seed. They crushed two matches 3–0 and 4–0, and faced Vancouver in the Stage 1 finals. Shock lost 3–4. They were now 0–2 in matches against Vancouver.

Counterintuitively, the Stage 1 finals loss increased Shock's confidence. Sinatraa explained their thinking, saying, "We knew if we could take the best team in the league to seven maps, then we must actually be good." In Stage 2, Shock weren't good; they were perfect. Shock won every Stage 2 match, and every map of every match, for a 7–0 match record and a 28–0 map record. The casters decided to call this a Golden Stage and predicted that it would never happen again (it would not, at least for the rest of the season). Titans also won every match of Stage 2 to remain undefeated, but they dropped three maps along the way. The Stage 2 final was a rematch of the Stage 1 final: San Francisco Shock versus Vancouver Titans. After the season, Sinatraa would cite this match—a particular play from this match, in fact—as his personal highlight. Four of his teammates fell in a team fight, taking only two Titans down with them. It was Sinatraa and Rascal versus four Titans, in other words, certain death. Sinatraa used his ultimate ability, known as Graviton Surge, which created a mini–black hole on the map, sucking enemies in and holding them there, which allowed Rascal to pick one off. Over the next twenty-two seconds, Sinatraa dealt enough damage to the remaining three Titans to completely recharge his ult. To appreciate the brilliance of his execution, you need to understand how this approaches the theoretical limits of the game: if all six of the opposing team were just standing still, a pro could probably get an ult charge in just under twenty seconds. The Titans were not standing still, and there were only three of them, and yet Sinatraa not only built back up to his ult but used it again to win the fight. Sinatraa would go on to have incredible moments during Season 2, but this was the moment he did something so transcendent in the game that it became lore: "the twenty-second Grav," as fans called it.

Shock would go on to win that map, and the match. The season score was now Shock 1, Titans 2, each with a stage championship (and $200,000 prize).

After the Stage 2 finals match, Sinatraa's mom bought two nonrefundable plane tickets to Philadelphia. The Grand Finals would be played in the Wells Fargo Center, home of the Philadelphia 76ers and Philadelphia Flyers. She didn't tell Sinatraa she bought them.

Shock would finish Stage 3 5–2 and again qualify for the stage playoffs. For the third time, they made it to the final. Only instead of meeting their old nemesis there, they would face the unlikely opponent, the Shanghai Dragons.

Any fan who'd followed Season 1 would have been astonished to know Dragons had made it this far. That team's reversal revealed just how turbulent the young league was. This was the team that went 0–40 in the 2018 season. How had they found their way to a stage final match?

The answer was that they, like many other teams, pushed the South Korea button. After their winless season, the Shanghai Dragons released six Chinese players, keeping one, Diya, and also keeping their lone South Korean player, Geguri. They then signed eight new players, all of them from South Korea. Geguri would not play in this match, as she'd been replaced in the Dragons lineup by yet another Boston castoff, Gamsu.

In the Stage 3 final, Shock got a little too cute on the first map, running an unusual composition on a last-second whim from Crusty, and they lost. Perhaps shaken, they then lost the next two maps, looking like an entirely different team, tentative in their moves, unsure. The score stood

3–0 in a best of seven series. On Map 4, Shock dominated, then won two tight maps to take the match to Map 7. As they clawed back from 0–3 to tie it up, they looked Golden again. They felt sure they were going to win: this was their season. Before Map 7, Sinatraa told his team that they were going to win. The Dragons won Map 7 easily.

This loss was devastating to Shock. The players had tears visible in their eyes as they high-fived Dragons after the match. Brett was also devastated. The fact that Shock was the only team to make it to all three stage final matches meant little to them. Brett couldn't see a bright side, at least not at that moment, and he definitely didn't want to talk about it.

The Overwatch League did something very strange after Stage 3, something I've never heard of in professional sports, or even esports: they fundamentally changed the rules of the game midseason. "Nate Nanzer never would have let this happen," Brett fumed to me. Nate had abandoned the Overwatch League after Stage 2 because Epic Games, the creators of *Fortnite*, had dumped a flying busload of money onto him, and he was now running *Fortnite*'s competitive esports operation.

The rule change that caused so much unease was called role lock. For all of the 2018 season and three quarters of the 2019 season, there were no rules about what composition a team ran. Six tanks, six damage, six supports, or any combination thereof was just fine. The most common composition during the 2018 dive meta was 2-2-2, but a new meta had emerged during 2019, a kind of gameplay referred to as GOATS. GOATS comp was named after the Contenders team that invented it, similar to how the spawn-camping strategy developed by Sinatraa, Dafran, and Dhak on Brad's Selfless team was known as Selfless comp. GOATS comp used three tanks and three supports, but unlike dive meta, there's no spreading out, or sending a Tracer to attack the back line, or positioning a Widowmaker on the high ground, or any type of strategic positioning at all. Instead, the team sticks very close together as a rolling ball of unkillable chaos, strengthened by the high health of the tanks combined with three healers.

The new challenge for every team became how to get kills against this strategy and defeat it, and the answer was coordination. Either everyone on your team must focus fire on the same member of the opposing team at the same time, or two players must use their ultimate abilities in combination.

The action that resulted from GOATS comp was, for me, fun to watch. I had always had a limited understanding of what was going on during the dive meta, as the game was just too fast for me to follow given the action often taking place at different parts of the map at the same time. In GOATS when Sinatraa would land a Graviton Surge that sucked the entire opposing team into one place as Choi sent D.Va's self-destructing mech into their midst, the result was immediately apparent and incredible. Everyone died. I could follow that.

But many Overwatch fans had a different reaction. Complaints about the GOAT comp were posted on reddit and various Blizzard forums, and the traditional sports people running OWL drew a direct line from GOATS comp to declining ratings during Season 2. Their solution was role lock.

From a general manager's perspective, it was an extraordinary headache. Brett had planned his entire year, in fact the past two years, on the assumption that his team could play whatever the best composition happened to be in any given meta. He had recruited and signed adaptable players, like Sinatraa, who could play damage heroes or tank heroes at the highest level. By instituting the role lock, teams with elite damage players who'd been riding the bench during GOATS gained a relative advantage, as their previously useless players were now essential. Case in point: Babybay, now playing for the Atlanta Reign. As a damage specialist, Babybay was a spot starter during the GOATS meta and then one of the best players in the league during Stage 4. In the same way that the buff to Mercy in the prior season had sent Dhak out of the league, role lock catapulted Babybay from the bench to the top of the league.

Led by Babybay's obscene damage output during Stage 4, the Atlanta Reign went undefeated and made the playoffs. Role lock didn't slow down Shock though: they also went undefeated, finishing the season second behind the

Vancouver Titans, at 23–5. "We led the league in map differential," Brett crowed. Though Titans had won two more matches than Shock during the season, because of their Golden Stage and tendency to 4–0 their opponents, Shock won three more maps.

To determine the five candidates for the league's Most Valuable Player award, first the general managers of all twenty OWL teams submitted ballots nominating five players who didn't play for them. After the votes were tallied, of the five MVP finalists, two were on Vancouver and two were on Shock: Sinatraa and Super. According to the twenty people whose job it was to scout and sign pro *Overwatch* players, the two kids who couldn't even play the first half of the 2018 season were now among the five best players in the world. To determine the Most Valuable Player, OWL used 25 percent votes from fans, 75 percent votes from press, coaches, general managers, casters, and analysts. They chose Sinatraa.

When the glow of the season had begun to wear off, I asked Sinatraa what winning the MVP award meant to him. "I want people to think that I'm good," he answered. "When they look up my name, I want to be considered the best. Winning MVP means I'm..." he paused, "I'm *one* of the best." He laughed. I knew why, because he was the best, but he didn't think he should. And he knew that I knew.

Over the course of the second season, Sinatraa had managed to harness the fierce competitiveness that had once caused people to consider him "toxic on Ladder." There was a change in his tone, if not in the contents, of his trash talk—he still regularly predicted "easy 4–0s" when asked by casters what they should expect in the next match.

I was fascinated to know how it was that he was able to transform his trash talk without coming across as malicious.

"Bro, are you asking me how I learned how to trash talk?" he responded. Clearly, it's inherent. It just needed some polish.

Shock's first playoff match was against a familiar face: Brad Rajani, now head coach of the Atlanta Reign, featuring star player Babybay. Shock and Reign had been the best teams in Stage 4, and it hadn't been particularly close. They both fielded damage gods along with stellar tank and support play. Other teams, tuned more for GOATS and not as adaptable as the Crusty-led Shock, couldn't keep up. Even the mighty Titans had dropped two matches—of only three games lost in their season—after the role lock was introduced.

The best change to Season 2 was to the regular-season playoffs, which became double elimination. Because of the new format and the utter dominance of Reign and Shock during Stage 4, the playoff match between them was considered a championship preview. Whichever team lost would likely emerge from the losers bracket for a championship rematch. Their match was one of the best of the season. The teams were evenly skilled, with Babybay going toe-to-toe with his former teammate, and newly minted MVP, Sinatraa. Reign took the first map, Shock took the second, and they continued one by one until the match was tied 3–3. On the seventh map, Shock, on offense first, had managed to push the cart nearly all the way to the end, on a map called Rialto, which looks a bit like Venice, Italy.

Rialto was very difficult on offense toward the end, as there was a choke point and defenders had columns to hide behind, but the team pushing the cart must come in through a courtyard that completely lacks cover. On their turn on offense, Reign had been crashing against Shock's defenses, inching the cart closer to the line that marked Shock's finish, until less than twenty seconds remained. In the middle of the final fight of the match, a fight that Shock were nearly certain to win, Shock forgot to keep a player close to the cart to block it from moving forward. They C9ed. In the biggest match of their season, on Map 7 of a seven-map series, they lost because of the most amateur mistake possible. According to Crusty, everyone cried.

Moth took it the hardest, in fact so hard that a new meme was born: Moth face. The players have cameras on them from all angles at all times during a match, and when Moth realized he'd forgotten to touch the cart, it looked like his soul had been sucked out of his body through his face. This was captured from many different angles, replayed during the post-match analysis, posted all over reddit and other forums, and then replayed again at the beginning of the broadcast for the next Shock match.

After only one playoff match, Shock found themselves in the losers bracket. They would have to win every match to meet the winner's bracket champion in the Grand Finals. In their first match in the losers bracket, Shock met their old foe: the London Spitfire. Spitfire had finished the season in seventh place. They'd had an up-and-down season, qualifying for only one stage playoff, in which they were bounced in the first round. The situation now was eerily similar to the year before: Spitfire were about to play what might be their last match of the season. After being in exactly this position, they'd shredded everyone on their way to a championship. On the other side, Sinatraa gathered his teammates around him in the dugout. He looked them in the eye one by one, and each time he said, "We're going to 4–0." He was deadly serious.

The best-of-seven match against Spitfire was not close. Shock won 4–0. After the match, Brett walked down to the dugout and upon encountering Sinatraa in the hallway, gave him a fist pound. The next match was against Stan Kroenke's Los Angeles Gladiators, which Shock won 4–0. After the match, Brett again encountered Sinatraa on the way to the dugout, and they repeated the fist pound. For the following match they would face off against the expansion team, the Hangzhou Spark, and Shock won 4–0. After the match, Sinatraa headed back toward the dugout until a page informed

Sinatraa lasers across the stage towards me, gives me a fist pound, and says 'We've still got more games next season.'" Then Sinatraa went backstage and hugged his mom, drying her tears with his shirt. She told him about buying the plane tickets after Stage 2. At some point the tears began streaming down his face, too.

The team held a press conference after the match, and Choi would be asked, given how often overlooked he was playing the tank role, how it felt to finally be recognized as the Grand Finals MVP. He said that he won the MVP only because his teammates put him in a position to succeed, and he was thankful to them for the award. The next question was directed at Andy, but he ignored it, saying, "Everybody here has had their big moment, but nobody would be here without Choi. That is the most clutch player in the league." Super referred to Choi as the most selfless player on the team, and Sinatraa said, "Choi's the best teammate I've ever had. He never gets tilted in scrims, and if people do get tilted, he always picks the environment back up."

Over the course of two seasons, I heard players, coaches, and managers refer again and again to this issue: getting tilted. There's usually only one cause of getting tilted—losing—but it manifests in many ways: surliness, bitterness, whining, selfishness, anger, and the like. It can also be more subtle, such as the perception that the player helps his team more than they help him. When general managers told me that they traded a player because he got tilted, they would swear me to secrecy: that reputation destroys careers, because one player with a negative attitude destroys a team. Nearly all of these players are teenagers, five or six years away from fully wired prefrontal cortexes. We should expect them to be tilted. When Sinatraa credited Choi for being able to pick up the environment, it wasn't a throw-away compliment: he was saying that Choi helped prevent the team from destroying itself. How appropriate, given the role that Choi played in the game, tank, whose job is to shield his teammates from destruction.

The family-like interpersonal dynamics of the team continued between Andy and Super, who saw questions primarily as opportunities to make fun of each other. At one point, Andy was listing off the great qualities that led him to sign these players: selfless, supportive, et cetera, finally saying of Super, "We could see an emerging Chad personality." This was a very weird thing to say. A Chad personality is a man who can be defined by the Wikipedia entry for alpha male. Someone disinterested in intellectual pursuits because he's already cracked the code: gym, tan, laundry. Andy was sort of saying that he saw an emerging leader in Super, but he was also sort of saying that Super lives an unexamined life. And he was using internet slang to do it. That had to be the weirdest thing that a team owner has ever said about one of their players just after winning a championship. It did not go unnoticed. After Andy finished, Super quickly chimed in with masterful timing and sarcasm, "Nice answer, Andy." The room laughed. Super had established dominance over Andy. Total Chad move.

Someone asked Shock whether they could do it again in 2020. Sinatraa answered, "With the depth of our roster, no matter what meta it is, we're always going to be on top." Then Crusty added, "And also, we have, really, the best coach in the world." This got laughs. Sinatraa and Crusty were a perfect match. Crusty praised his assistant coaches, JunkBuck and NineK, saying he felt like the team had three head coaches. The bravado was warranted. In 2019, Shock played twenty-eight regular-season matches and sixteen playoff matches. Of their forty-four total matches, they won thirty-seven (84 percent win rate, equivalent to a 13–3 NFL team), but more astonishingly, they won twenty-four of their matches 4–0 (55 percent). Imagine an NFL team holding the opposing team to zero points or an MLB team pitching a no-hitter every other game. Toward the end of the press conference, Andy referred to Shock as a dynasty. It's not a crazy idea. The average age of this team was nineteen years old, meaning this exact roster could theoretically contend for a championship for the next eight years. Of course, that's only from a physical standpoint. How they bear up under the mental pressure of reigning world champions is another matter. A week after the Championship,

Sinatraa and Super would appear on *The Tonight Show Starring Jimmy Fallon*. During the 2019 World Cup, Sinatraa would lead the US team to its first championship. Sinatraa would be named MVP. Sinatraa, the toxic Ladder kid, mama's boy, Mr. $150K, and reigning MVP, was now the face of American esports. What would become of him?

Tens of thousands of hours of teamwork, sitting side by side in the house, speaking directly into each other's ears through the headsets. A thousand meals shared and hundreds of nights spent sleeping under the same roof, just down the hall from one another. A hundred weekend days spent doing the same things together every other teenager does—shopping for shoes and watching Avengers movies. *Overwatch* requires an insane level of teamwork. It moves so fast with such complexity, requiring every player on the team to be simultaneously playing offense and defense at every moment. The chance of winning is weighted so heavily on a team's ability to anticipate each other that maybe the only way to win is to form that bond away from the game. There's no going home to a family or a girlfriend. Home has to be in the gamer house, and family has to be your teammates. When Sinatraa told me that Shock didn't need to scout Vancouver's players or strategies ahead of the finals, he wasn't being overconfident or dismissive. He was just saying something true: "We knew that if we just focused on *our* team, we could beat anyone who showed up that day."

ACKNOWLEDGMENTS

This book's existence depended on the suspended disbe-lief of three people: the writer, the publisher, and Brett Lautenbach. I had to believe I could write it, David Lamb had to believe that publishing it was a good idea, and Brett had to believe both of those things.

I did not believe in myself as a writer until I met Sam Kashner. I heard about Sam nearly every day for months before I met him. He'd been regaling my at-the-time girl-friend with stories while he ate breakfast at Café Gitane, where she worked. I would later hear these stories second-hand, in a somewhat jealous mindset, as Sam's stories were terribly interesting, and even worse he was a bestselling author. I finally met Sam in a hospital lobby on Christ-mas Eve in Manhattan in 2012 or so. Sam's arm was in a sling, as he'd broken it slipping on ice, but he still wanted

Acknowledgments

to hug me as he'd heard so much about me and was so excited to meet me. This didn't seem like the behavior of a man intent on stealing my girlfriend. And besides, his broken arm was really the fault of Johnny Depp, Hunter S. Thompson, and a pair of sensible shoes that were certainly not "shit-kicking boots" as required of guests to Thompson's funeral, which was hosted by Jonny Depp, who wore the same size shoe as Sam. Sam first donned Mr. Depp's shoes as he watched Mr. Thompson's remains get shot out of a cannon, and then off and on for many years until that very night. This story was eminently implausible, and I was immediately charmed. Sam and I became friends, and eventually I got the courage up to admit to him my dirty secret: I'd always wanted to be a writer. He was thrilled to hear this. He edited my first attempt at a magazine column, which was not accepted for publication, and led me to the excellent William LoTurco, my literary agent, who convinced me that perhaps there was a book here. Sam has remained thrilled for me, providing intellectual and artistic support throughout this book project and the many false starts and detours that led to publication. I never would have even tried this without Sam.

I originally submitted to David Lamb a very different book proposal, one which David and thirty other New York publishers agreed was not good. David was the only one who saw something and encouraged me to submit a second one to him, which led to this book. I could not have written this book without him. He knew he was getting a first-time writer, yet expectations could not have been low enough. He had to condense a college writing education into a few hours on the phone, and edit out numerous wild tangents about Urban Meyer's moral compass or the time I rampaged through Stockholm with the esports godfathers or whatever passed through my mind when I got to that page. I know it wasn't easy, because I was there for all of it. Thankfully David has talent, but more importantly David once wanted to go pro in Halo. Only a true believer would work that hard to get this project across the finish line.

It wouldn't have gone anywhere, though, without Brett Lautenbach. Having a writer around can be dangerous, he must have known—who knows what my agenda is or how I might interpret events?—but that didn't stop him. I have to think that Brett's childhood dream of making movies had something to do with his willingness to put himself on the line for me and this book… Brett took an immediate risk by vouching for me to his boss, Andy Miller, whose blessing I needed to get started. Andy was incredibly open about why he'd gotten into the business, the financial calculus behind the investment, his love of competition and sports, and why he loved Brett. In those first conversations, Brett and Andy told me those values and culture were at

Acknowledgments

the top of the stack. They were willing to bring on Brad Rajani, based as much on the fact that he's a great dude as on his ability to scout talent. They were willing to sign two seventeen-years-olds, Sinatraa and Super, because the focus was on building a lasting organization, or as Andy put it after winning the Season Two Championship, a dynasty. That dynasty is a much a credit to Brett as anyone. I can understand how he attracted and inspired his coaches and players so well—even with me, he was always generous with his time, despite that every hour spent with me was one less hour of sleep.

Jack Etienne built Cloud9 into the most valuable esports org in the world in part through a similar openness—Jack loves mixing it up with fans on reddit and Twitter—but just as much because he's a gamer through and through. When I sat down with him for our formal, on the record interview, I asked how he'd been spending his time lately. In the last week he'd blasted through three RPGs. That's how Jack recharges. Jack let me behind the scenes of the Spitfire for the playoff run with full knowledge that the team was in turmoil. They'd fired their coach, stumbled into the playoffs, and there was incredible tension and pressure on the team. This was the type of situation in which most owners would say, "now is not a good time." Jack didn't say that. Perhaps instinctively, or perhaps because he trusts his people, and because his General Manager,

Acknowledgments

Susie Kim, vouched for me, he said OK. He also bought me a $100 steak.

The first time I met Susie was when she hopped into the press room to exclaim over the intensity of the current Spitfire match. She shared the type of insight I love—what's really going on in the match, based on the relationships and emotional states of the players working together onstage. Her enthusiasm was infectious, and after striking out with the top two seeded teams in the play-offs, I decided to follow my heart and ask Susie if I could tag along with the Spitfire. She heard me out, pitched the idea to Jack, and that's how I found myself in the underbelly of the Barclay's Center for the first ever Overwatch League Grand Finals. Susie's story is incredible: an initially heart-rending, ultimately inspiring international journey leading to a secret romance with a famous esports caster. Susie's now-husband, Christopher Mykles, better known as MonteCristo, welcomed me behind the scenes on the casting side of the league. His insights were invaluable to this book, and anything that's wrong I probably just forgot to check with him. Susie and Monte welcomed me behind the scenes and into their lives, inviting me to their wedding and dinners at their beautiful home. The story of their romance remains to be told, as including it in the word count it deserves was beyond the scope of this book. I hope at least that Susie's warmth and thoughtful,

Acknowledgments

analytical mind have come through. Without Susie, I would have missed how a South Korean team operates behind the scenes (very similarly, with more complaining about American food), and how the players handled the pressure of a championship match right there in their little tiny locker room in the hours before the match. It's not that important whether or not I perfectly captured Monte, as you can get the full experience for yourself on his Overwatch League show, *Watchpoint.*

After the Shock released him, Brad Rajani sat down with me for three hours to fill in the details of his journey from '90s esports pro to OWL coach. He didn't have to do that, he already had the Atlanta head coaching job, but he went out of his way to help me, and that was characteristic throughout the season. He was always willing to explain why the team attempted certain strategies, why those hadn't worked, why Babybay was in Puerto Rico, or whatever else I wanted to know.

Crusty was exactly the same—open and honest. He may even be the most direct person I've ever met. In the book he's presented as an OWL mastermind, which he absolutely is, but he's also a light-hearted goofball who makes his players run through sprinklers in between scrims. I've forgotten more of what Crusty taught me about Overwatch than a Silver level player ever deserved to learn.

The players on the Shock were great. I'm twice the age

of the most of them, but they didn't make me feel like a weirdo for watching them and writing things about them in my little notebook. I found it very hard to be the "fly on the wall" I'd promised to be, as the conversations were often impossible to resist. It's tough for humor to translate to a general reader when the jokes are so inside this world, but I hope their humor shines through—and where it doesn't, readers should know that these guys are great company, and very funny. Super and Sinatraa are champion shit-talkers, and generally hilarious company, as are Babybay, Iddqd, Nomy, Dhak, Sleepy and Danteh. (The two players I've savagely left off that list, Nevix and Moth, are two of the kindest and most earnest people I've ever met.) I'll remain a fan of all of them whichever team they find themselves on. While I didn't get to know the Spitfire players as well, or the new players added to the Shock from Korea (due to both the language barrier and the shorter time with them), they never treated me like the outsider I was, and I'm grateful for that. They bummed me cigarettes, and let me listen to them talk, with Susie or Robin translating, or sometimes not.

Even with all these appreciations, I haven't come close to naming all the people who helped me. Nobody had to do any of this. I don't think anyone who was involved was angling for any sort of benefit from the book: they just wanted me to understand their world, to learn to love it